S&A Links
c. 1910

Southport and Ainsdale:
The Golfers' Club
1906 -2006

RYDER CUP
OFFICIAL
SOUVENIR PROGRAMME

PRICE 1/-

THE FOURTH INTERNATIONAL GOLF MATCH
GREAT BRITAIN *versus* THE UNITED STATES OF AMERICA
TO BE PLAYED ON THE SOUTHPORT AND AINSDALE COURSE,
SOUTHPORT
ON MONDAY AND TUESDAY JUNE 26·27, 1933

This Official Programme is published by the Professional Golfers' Association and the proceeds will be devoted
to the British Ryder Cup Fund.

Ryder Cup Programme 1933

Southport and Ainsdale: The Golfers' Club 1906 -2006

By
Harry Foster

917/1080

Southport and Ainsdale Golf Club 2006

Southport and Ainsdale Golf Club 2006

**First published in the United Kingdom in 2006 by
The Southport and Ainsdale Golf Club,
Southport.**

ISBN 0-9552540-0-0

Typeset in 11 on 13pt New Baskerville
and printed in Great Britain by
Custom Print Limited
13-23 Naylor Street, Liverpool, England.

Published for Southport and Ainsdale Golf Club by
Custom Print Limited, England.

Southport and Ainsdale: The Golfers' Club 1906-2006

Published in a limited edition of 1,000 copies

Copy Number

Harry Foster

Custom Print, England 2006

ACKNOWLEDGEMENTS

In 1946, the Captain - J.A. Sloan – presciently asked Walter Childs, one of the founder members, to write down his early memories of the Club. This he did and the document, a draft of which was checked by Charles Leigh the Club's first honorary secretary, provides a valuable insight into these early years. It also serves as an illustration of the fallibility of memory when accounts of events are compared with the contemporary evidence in minute books and newspapers. Child's manuscript provided the basis for Stan Dickinson's brief unfinished account of the Club's early history. Documents left by Geoff Roberts provide a personal account of life at S&A during his long association with the Club, particularly in relation to competitive golf. Geoff had started to organise these memoirs into a coherent form, a task that he was sadly unable to complete. Vernon Cubbon has proved to be a dedicated custodian of these papers and other archive material at S&A. The late Dorothy Ritchie, then gloriously in her nineties, undertook to collect material for a chapter on the ladies' section, with enthusiasm and energy. Rita Ritchie, who recorded the contents of the ladies' honours' boards, assisted her.

In addition to these written contributions, S&A is fortunate in having retained all the minutes of the Board and of the various committees. To consult this vast archive I have repeatedly sought the co-operation of Carol Birrell and her team, during what has been an unsettled period. They, I am sure, will be glad to see the back of me, but they were unfailingly warm and generous in their welcome.

Sympathetic technical help always plays a large part in the production of a book. Derek Holden has provided some of the photographs, including the one on the jacket. Many images from the Club's rich photographic collection have been copied by Eric Page and Tony Crane. Chris Driver has employed his computer expertise to enhance some low-grade images. Art-work to replace a poor early newspaper photograph is by my son David. As always my wife Thelma has contributed to the task of proof reading and acted as a sounding board.

I am also grateful to the many members and others who have provided me with material and information. These have included Hilary Ambrose, Gill Appleton, Errol Cheesman, Vernon Cubbon, Tim Culshaw, John Donoghue, Michael Edwards, Graham Fisher, Brian Gill, John Graham, Alan Harrison, Pat Henshaw, Keith Hick, Paul Hiley, Mike Houghton, Stan Jackson, Peter Lennon, Jack McLachlan, Harry Mann, David Marsh, Mike Mercer, Ted Minoprio, George Mitchell, Linda Nolte, Liz O'Rourke, Jim Payne, Alan Ravey, Mark Rawlinson, Ken Ritchie, Pat Roberts, Jim Robinson, Tony Rodwell, Southport Reference Library, George Tomlinson, Peter Wilding, Jackie Wroe, Women Golfers' Museum (Edinburgh), and principally the Club Historian Tony Crane. Although a number of helping hands have contributed to the writing of this history, I accept complete responsibility for its form and contents. Attempting to chronicle a hundred years in a limited number of pages means that some events and personalities will have been omitted, but I hope that all readers will gain a sense of what a great club this is.

Harry Foster

Contents

Preface

The Captain - Mr. Paul Gwynne

To be elected Captain of Southport and Ainsdale Golf Club is indeed a privilege and to be chosen as Captain in our Centenary Year is a very special honour. I joined S&A in 1964 at the age of ten and will forever be grateful to my late mother for paying the sum of five pounds for my first year's subscription. Through golf I have had the opportunity to meet hundreds of golfers and have made a significant number of life-long friends; for this, I will always be indebted to S&A.

Over the years there have been constant improvements to both the course and the clubhouse. Our course is consistently rated in the top ten courses in the United Kingdom by all the leading golf magazines, and *Golf World* has rated S&A in its top ten list of the best qualifying courses for the British Open. The present clubhouse was built in 1926 and has been developed and modernised over the years to give us facilities to match the excellence of the course. Our close association with the R&A has always been important to S&A and we are pleased to have been chosen as hosts for the British Mid-Amateur Championship during our Centenary Year.

I would like to thank all the members of the Centenary Committee in making 2006 an historical and memorable year. The Lady Captain, Carol Fitzgibbon, and I look forward to a joyous year with our families, friends and members of S&A.

Finally a special thank you to Dr. Harry Foster, we are privileged to have such a fine author for our centenary book. Also thanks to past captain Vernon Cubbon and Club Historian Tony Crane for their efforts to assemble and provide proper custodial care for the Club's archives, so that the Club's collection of photographs and memorabilia can now be displayed in the clubhouse, for the benefit of members and visitors.

Good Golfing.

Paul Gwynne

The Lady Captain
Mrs. Carol Fitzgibbon

It was with great pleasure that I accepted the invitation to be Lady Captain in the Centenary Year.

The lady members are very proud to be part of and to have contributed to the success of our renowned golf club.

Throughout this special year a variety of celebrations and activities have been planned. Hoping that all members will enjoy these, reflect on the friendships and achievements of the Club over the past hundred years, and look forward to its continued success.

Carole Fitzgibbon

Introduction

Almost with one consent, the landowners of the Liverpool district have united in offering facilities for golf, rightly recognising a golf club as a nucleus of a residential estate. The railway companies are following suit. Golfers pay ground rents in one case, and take contract tickets in the other. As the houses multiply, there is no end to the revenue of the ground landlord or of the Railway Company. Small wonder, then, that both these monopolists recognise in golf a sort of beneficent farming who use the deserts of sand.
Southport Visiter March 1904

On Whit Saturday afternoon 1906, fifty-one golfers gathered for an inaugural mixed competition on a small crudely laid out nine-hole course on Birkdale Common. These members of the newly created Grosvenor Golf Club made sand tees on each of the holes, and then simultaneously drove off. The Club, which was soon to become Southport and Ainsdale, was officially open.

Southport and Ainsdale is now one of an extraordinary cluster of internationally famous championship golf links on the south-west Lancashire coast. Henry Longhurst described this area as '…a sandy paradise that stretches for miles along the coast between Liverpool and Southport.' For Bernard Darwin it was '…a noble stretch of golfing ground that is second to none.' The golf clubs have justifiably earned the coast its reputation as 'The Mecca of Golf' and 'The Golf Coast'. Both Southport and Ainsdale and Royal Birkdale have twice hosted Ryder Cup matches with the United States; Royal Birkdale is a regular venue for the Open Championship; whilst all the links along this coast have for many years staged major championships and representative matches, both amateur and professional.

South-west Lancashire boasts the largest and arguably the finest tract of coastal sand dunes in the country. The strip is over ten miles long and a mile in depth. Sand dunes are only found adjoining gently shelving beaches. In Lancashire, large areas of sand are exposed at low tide and the prevailing wind blows the sun-dried sand inland to form a sand dune system. On the tall outer hills marram grass, locally called 'starr', struggles to stabilize them, but the vegetation cover is not complete and the wind can quickly reshape these 'mobile' dunes. Further inland the dunes become completely covered by vegetation. Lime derived from shells helps to promote plant growth. Local farmers were able to extract a crop even from this unpromising land.

They developed warrens to farm rabbits for flesh and fur. Where the vegetation cover is thin, the wind can form deep hollows down to the water table. Initially these hollows, or 'slacks', are wet all the year round. Many later build up to form dry slacks, which are still damp enough to support abundant plant life. Further inland dune heath develops. Here the soil has been impoverished by rain leaching down such nutrients that the sand did contain. Local farmers developed special techniques to cultivate the poor soil of this marginal land. A feature of the landscape was the small fields, which were known as 'heys', the old English word for enclosure. The fields were enclosed with banks or 'cops' of earth several feet tall. In addition to acting as field boundaries, cops also protected the light sandy soil from being carried away by the strong prevailing winds. This was particularly important when there was seed on the ground. Hedge planting on the cops, a requirement in some local leases, increased their effectiveness as windbreaks, and the roots served to stabilize them. These cops featured as hazards on some of the early golf courses. Although many have been removed at Southport and Ainsdale, the remnants of such field cops are still visible on the 3rd, 4th, 9th, 11th, 12th and 13th holes (Fig.1). By the time that golf courses were being developed much of the dune heath land was being used as pasture to provide milk for the residents of the rapidly growing neighbouring suburbs.

It was the building of a railway line from Liverpool to Southport in the middle of the nineteenth century, which was to transform this previously sparsely populated coastal strip. The middle classes were quitting their suburbs on the immediate fringes of the city, fleeing both the smoke and the remorseless advance of Liverpool's people-teeming terraces. The availability of regular and rapid transport into the heart of city meant that the land along this northern line became an attractive proposition for commuters. Nature contributed fresh, clean air and the landowners ensured that the new suburbs offered the social seclusion so valued by the middle classes.

Members of the Liverpool business community, who had strong Scottish connections, brought the 'Royal and Ancient Game' to the north-west coast. They initially played on 'The Warren' at Hoylake, an area cropped by sheep and rabbits. The Liverpool Golf Club, later Royal Liverpool, was founded there in 1869. The first club to be formed along the railway line on the northern bank of the Mersey was the West Lancashire Club at Blundellsands, which was founded in 1873. Formby Golf Club was formed in 1884 and played on 'The Warren' at Freshfield. A month later the Southport (Hesketh) Golf Club followed on the Marshside Hills, the northern end of the dune coast, where sandhills give way to Ribble marshes. This club was

1. Remnants of field cops on the 12th hole at S&A. (See Fig.59)

2. Sand dunes north of Shore Road. This is the land rejected by the Banking and Insurance Golf Club. Ainsdale-on-Sea Railway Station and the Lakeside Hotel are in the foreground..

3. The bunker-surrounded green of the 'Cottage Hole' (15th) on the Banking and Insurance (Freshfield) Course 1933. Like S&A, this course was laid out on dune heath.

born out of the local social elite and it was members of this group who four years later also formed the Birkdale Club, with a course on land belonging to Charles Weld-Blundell, who owned all the land in Birkdale and Ainsdale.

At about the turn of the century Weld-Blundell was putting his energies into an attempt to develop Ainsdale-on-Sea as a high-class residential area. He believed that a golf course, north of Shore Road between the Lancashire and Yorkshire Railway and the Cheshire Lines Railway, would give an impetus to the sluggish rate of residential growth. An article in the *Southport Visiter* in March 1904 noted:

> Mr. Weld-Blundell has been credited with a natural desire to see a golf club founded at Ainsdale, which like nothing else, would ensure its rapid development given the Lancashire and Yorkshire Railway expresses and the Cheshire Lines Railway expresses and a golf course. Manchester and Warrington gentlemen would find it a capital golfing place, where golf would give social advantages, sought amongst country and seaside residents.

His problem at Ainsdale was that there were not sufficient local middle-class residents to sponsor a course. Nevertheless, in 1906 it appeared that he had found an unusual prospective tenant to develop one. Members of the Liverpool banking and insurance community had been holding golf competitions and were attempting to establish their own club. They obtained an option to secure land at Ainsdale-on-Sea that was virtually a southwards continuation of the links of the Birkdale Golf Club. Weld-Blundell offered them the recently built Lakeside Hotel, in Shore Road, as a clubhouse and the railways were prepared to allow golfers reduced rates for season tickets (Fig.2). At a meeting to put the scheme to members, the principal organiser described Weld-Blundell as '...a generous landowner with a zeal for the improvement of his residential estate by the most modern means, the multiplication of golf clubs.' The verdict of the majority was, however, a thumbs down on this site. They claimed that the tall scrub covered dunes were too daunting a hazard for novice golfers. Being prudent men of finance, they also recognised the potential high cost of '...drainage and turfage'. After further negotiations with Weld-Blundell they eventually leased an area of dune heath between Ainsdale and Freshfield in 1908. This land was more easily converted into a golf course (Fig.3). The Banking and Insurance Golf Club, whose clubhouse was close to Freshfield Station, later changed its name to Freshfield Golf Club, which was to lose its course to the Air Ministry for the construction of Woodvale aerodrome during World War II.

Thus in 1906, the year of the formation of the Grosvenor Golf Club, there were already two well established golf clubs in the area (the Hesketh, formerly Southport, and the Birkdale Clubs) and the prospect of a third (the Banking and Insurance Club).

PART ONE
1906-1939

Chapter One

THE BEGINNINGS: THE GROSVENOR GOLF CLUB

Prior to the establishment of the Grosvenor Club there were two well-established clubs in Southport, whose entrance fees and subscriptions were much in excess of those in other provincial towns, and far in excess of those necessary to maintain a really first-class golf club.

Southport Visiter October 1906

The Grosvenor Golf Club was initially little influenced by Charles Weld-Blundell, even though it was on his land. Notes written forty years after the founding of the Club by one of the original members indicate that the golf club had its origins in a whist club - the Grosvenor Club. The author, Walter Child, did not say where this club met, but it seems that it might have been at the Smedley Hotel on the corner of Grosvenor Road and York Road. Later advertisements for this hotel show that a Grosvenor Bridge Club met there. What is known is that by January 1906 some members of the whist club, both male and female, were considering the possibility of establishing a new golf club in Birkdale. It was agreed that six of the men, who knew something about the game, should seek further information on how they might proceed. Within a couple of weeks a meeting of those members with an interest in the project was called. Forty-two turned up to hear the group's recommendations and it was unanimously decided that the group of six should be elected to act as a committee. Its brief was '...to further investigate the possibility of creating a golf course', and the committee was given authority to take whatever action it deemed to be necessary to expedite matters. Serving notice of its future tactics the committee did just that.

In February an agreement was reached to lease part of Peter Lloyd's Hill Side (sic.) Farm, which was situated immediately inland of the railway line on the approach to Birkdale Common. It was a thirty-acre triangle of mainly cultivated dune heath. Bounded on one side by the railway, it stretched from what we now know as Conyers Avenue, extended as far inland as Blundell Drive, and reached as far south as the area of Hillside Station (Fig.4). The land consisted of a mixture of grass-covered sandhills and of rough flatter pastures. Lloyd grazed his cows on this land, and as was

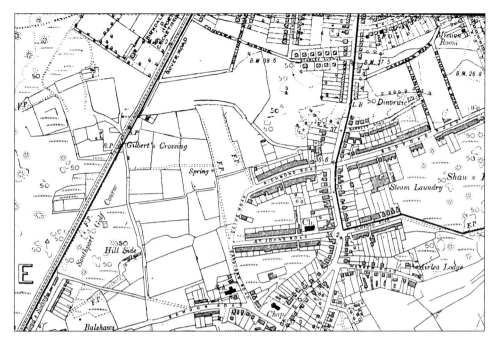

4. The Grosvenor (Southport) Golf Club Course 1906. Lloyd's Hill Side Farm is shown along with the cottages of Lloyd's Siding, which were to the south of where Hillside Station now stands.

common in the district, low earth banks - 'cops' - surrounded small fields. During the next three months some of the members, assisted by Lloyd, fashioned this land into a rudimentary nine-hole golf course. Knowledge of its layout is limited, but Child described it as being '...as rough an outlay as was ever played on.' Field cops were utilised as hazards in front of greens and '...were designated as bunkers', thus players had to '...learn to pitch...there could be no running-up.' Flat areas had been identified for greens, and these small mown areas were surrounded by a rail of posts and wires to protect them from grazing cattle. The cropping of the grass by these beasts was the only attention received by the rest of the ground that made up the nine holes. There were probably narrow gaps in the fences around the 'greens' so that ladies wearing long skirts could pass thorough. Miss Willcock, one of the original members, later recalled that jam pots were initially used as holes.

Child did describe one of the holes - the 5th. It was the longest on the course, measuring about 400 yards, and was played to a small, elevated green placed in a saucer-shaped depression on the top of a conical sandhill. This green was in the hilly south-west corner of the course close to a now demolished terrace of labourers' houses, which was known as Lloyd's Siding.

It was situated alongside the railway, south of where Hillside Station now stands (Fig.5). The green was only about eighteen feet in diameter and the slope of the hill fell away sharply in all directions. Under hit your approach and the ball would roll back, but a strong shot would finish over the green in '...a huge bed of docks, nettles and weeds which grew there in an impenetrable mass.' Such rough also occurred in other areas of the course. A small wooden hut with a verandah in front, which had belonged to a nearby bowling club, was obtained and repaired by members for use as a pavilion. Measuring only about fifteen feet by twelve feet it offered the minimum in the way of facilities. It was erected at the entrance to the course, which was close to the railway by Gilbert's Crossing. This was alongside Birkdale's original long-closed railway station, which had been sited to serve the agricultural community on Birkdale Common.

By June 1906 the course was ready and the club, with over a hundred members, held its inaugural event. Child gives a detailed account of this mixed meeting held on the 'gloriously sunny' Whit Saturday afternoon. He reports that twenty-seven ladies and twenty-four men took part. As was

5. A distant view of the original course from the new course c.1910.
The terrace of cottages at Lloyd's Siding is visible on the left.
Hill Side farm can be seen in the trees. Note the small cop-surrounded fields of the heys.

6. F.W. Smith, S&A's first captain.

common in new golf clubs during this era, it seems that the majority of the members were golfing novices. As a consequence many wore clothing which looked as if it was normally reserved for gardening, and they shared a limited selection of golf clubs. Charles Leigh, an accountant and the first honorary secretary of the Club, organised the players into mixed three-balls, attempting to leaven the groups by spreading the more experienced golfers amongst the absolute beginners. There was a shotgun-style start, and an indication of the level of proficiency of the players was the fact that the nine-hole round, on this small course, took approximately four hours to complete. Air shots and mishits abounded and significantly the account in the *Southport Visiter* contained no results. After this 'competition' refreshments were taken in the hut. It seems that there was insufficient crockery and tea had to be served in relays. It was a quarter to eight, after the tea urn had finally been cleared from the small trestle table, before the Club's first captain – Mr. F.W. Smith – addressed the members, welcoming them and declaring the Grosvenor Golf Club officially launched (Fig.6).

Two days later, on Whit-Monday, the Club held its first men's handicap competition, and the published results indicate that the members included a core of experienced and proficient golfers. One of the thirty competitors was Walter Sugg, who had formerly played county cricket for Derbyshire and already had a golf handicap of four. There were several other players with handicaps of less than ten, and J.H. Bush won the event with a score of nett 80 off a handicap of five. In July there was a field of twenty-three for the first monthly medal. It was played on what the *Southport Visiter* described as a '…much extended and improved course.' In this first summer, Walter Sugg established himself as the Club's premier golfer. 'Long straight brassie shots' were apparently his trademark. He demonstrated his superiority over the field in the October medal when he scored a nett 71, with the runner-up trailing nine shots behind. By this time another competent golfer, Sidney J.F. Murphy a low single figure handicap member of the West Lancashire Club, had joined Grosvenor as his second club.

Walter Sugg and his brother Frank, a former Lancashire county cricket player who later joined the Club, ran a sports' outfitting business with a local branch on Lord Street, and others in Liverpool, Sheffield, Leeds and Cardiff. An advert in the *Southport Visiter* shows their company offering golf clubs, bags and balls for sale, with bargain sets for beginners. This was the period when the rubber-cored wound Haskell type of ball was replacing the old moulded gutta-percha 'gutties', the first having arrived from America in 1901. The Suggs offered Haskell balls at twenty-two shillings (£1.10p) a dozen, whereas the same number of remade gutties could be had for six shillings (30p). Child, a Scot and a marine engineer, noted that although most of the Grosvenor members used a gutty, he chose to play with a wound ball but kept a gutty for use on the short holes, because '…it didn't run in the same way'.

Although the Club was successful in attracting members (by October 1906 there were 140), and was financially sound, it faced three major problems. The first was identified in the *Southport Visiter* report of the initial Whit-Monday meeting. This included the statement that '…it is expected that the course will be shortly enlarged.' The course was already congested, particularly at weekends. But the present and projected increase of housing in the area meant that there was little scope for expansion on this site. Although some of the members might have been content to continue to play golf on this limited and rather primitive course, there was a dominant group whose members had ambitions to improve on this. The Committee called a meeting of members in October in order to consider the question of a completely new course. It was obviously felt that there was room for a third club in the town, which could provide and maintain a first-class course without needing to be as expensive as the well-established Southport and Birkdale clubs. The members were told that all the initial expenses had been met and that the Club still had a substantial balance.

A recommendation from the Committee to take a suggested new course was agreed unanimously. In fact, prior to this meeting the Committee had already held confidential, if unauthorised, negotiations with Mr. Skitt, the agent for the Weld-Blundell Estate and '…a very suitable piece of land' had been identified. It was '…situated between the first accumulator house on the Lancashire and Yorkshire Railway and Birkdale Cemetery.' (See front endpaper) George Lowe, the professional at Lytham had already inspected this land and prepared a provisional plan for a course to measure 5,600 yards. Construction work was started in the October of 1906 and Lowe was paid ten guineas (£10.50) for his services.

Records show that, although not drawing many members from upper middle-class Birkdale Park, the Club was attracting professional men and successful businessmen as members. For example, two of the leading seven players in the September medal were doctors, and at least two other members served on the councils of local authorities. The entrepreneurial drive of the pioneers, who had quickly moved this infant club from being tenants on a primitive nine-hole course, into being lessees of land for an eighteen-hole layout, on which a substantial clubhouse was to be built, prompted them to seek a change in the Club's status. After two extraordinary general meetings held in December it was '...unanimously decided that a limited liability company be formed of the members of the club, each member, present or future, to be a shareholder to the extent of at least one ordinary share. Debentures also to be issued.' The bulk of the shares were Ordinary Shares of one pound, there were also a limited number of five pounds Preference Shares, holders of which enjoyed the privilege of avoiding any future rise in subscriptions (Fig.7). A.N. Ross, a town councillor and a solicitor, had acted as chairman at some of the earlier meetings of members, but the Board of the new Company, which consisted of the members of the original committee, elected F.W. Dixon as its first chairman in February 1907. Charles Leigh was appointed as secretary, at an annual salary of twenty-five guineas (£26.25).

The question of a new clubhouse was left in abeyance. The Club would obviously have preferred a clubhouse close to a railway station, as was the case at the West Lancashire and Formby clubs. In 1904 the successful Liverpool to Southport commuter line had become the first steam railway in the world to be changed entirely to electric traction, and the Board decided to wait to see if the railway company was prepared to build a new station between Birkdale and Ainsdale.

The second issue facing the Club was that of playing rights. Although the ladies were associate members paying only a half fee, they were initially allowed full playing rights, an unusual arrangement for a golf club. There was a strong element of a 'social' club in this first year of its existence and a number of Saturday mixed golfing events were held, including a 'golf garden party'. Walter Suggs and his daughter won several of the mixed events. She was the Southport champion of the then fashionable game of ping-pong (table tennis). In August there was a ladies' competition on a Saturday, although ladies' medals were later held on weekdays. Nevertheless, ladies had the right to play at the weekends and apparently used it. It was at the weekends that the small course was most congested with

The Southport & Ainsdale Golf Club, Ltd.

Incorporated under the Companies Acts 1862-1900

REGISTERED OFFICE—13, POST OFFICE AVENUE. SOUTHPORT.

ISSUE OF 300 DEBENTURE BONDS OF FIVE POUNDS EACH.

Carrying Interest at the rate of Five Pounds per centum per annum, all ranking pari passu and numbered 1 to 300

No. 19   DEBENTURE BOND.   £5.

1. For the valuable consideration already received The Southport and Ainsdale Golf Club, Limited, (hereinafter called "the Company") will pay the Principal Moneys hereby secured at the time and in the events provided by the Conditions endorsed hereon to *Ernest Alfred Dixon*

of *36 Duke Street, Southport*

or other the Registered Holder for the time being hereof the sum of **Five Pounds**

2. The Company will in the meantime pay to such Registered Holder Interest thereon at the rate of Five Pounds per centum per annum by half-yearly payments on the First day of October and the First day of April in each year, the first of such half-yearly payments to be made on the First day of October next.

3. The Company hereby charges with such payments its undertaking and all its property, whatsoever and wheresoever, both present and future, including its uncalled capital for the time being.

4. This Debenture Bond is issued subject to the Conditions endorsed hereon which are to be deemed part of it.

Given under the Common Seal of the Company this *12th* day of *April* 19*07*

The Common Seal of the Company was affixed hereto in the presence of

C. Leigh
Secretary.

H W Smith
Walter Ivy

Directors

Copy.

Certificate of the Registration of a Series of Debentures where there is no trust Deed.

Pursuant to s. 14 (6) of the Companies Act, 1900 (63 and 64 Vict. c. 48).

Application having this day been made for the entry on the Register of the particulars required by sub-section 4 of section 14 of the Companies Act, 1900, in relation to a series of Debentures containing a charge (to the benefit of which the debenture holders of the said series are entitled *pari passu* created by the SOUTHPORT & AINSDALE GOLF CLUB, LTD., by resolution passed on the 20th day of February, 1907, (and one of such debentures dated within twenty-ne days of this date having been produced) **I hereby certify** that the total amount secured or intended to be secured by the said series is £1,500, and hat all the particulars required by sub-section 4 of section 14 of the said Act in relation to the said series have been this day entered on the Register.

Given under my hand at London this twelfth day of March, One thousand nine hundred and seven.

H. F. BARTLETT,

Registrar of Joint Stock Companies.

7. A Debenture Bond issued to E.A. Dixon in April 1907.

gentlemen players. The men's competitions were played on Saturdays and the result was confusion, competition for tee reservations and it seems that there were some bitter public arguments on the course. An exacerbating factor in promoting the tension between the sexes could well have been the relative levels of golfing proficiency at this time. In the ladies' December medal Mrs. Smith won with a gross score of 166-35 = 131, whilst in the first Captain's Prize event Miss L. Taylor, who appears to have been the Club's most consistently successful lady golfer, scored 126-30 = 96, which was both the best gross and the best nett score. Miss Rushton, who played off thirteen, appears to have held the lowest handicap. The notice convening the extra-ordinary general meeting of 5th December, which had been called to discuss finance, included the phrase '…and to discuss general business.' The major business went through almost on the nod, and it was the question of ladies' playing rights that dominated the meeting. Child reported that: 'There was much acrimonious discussion, motivated particularly by the ladies. However, after a stormy twenty-five minutes, a schedule of ladies' starting times was put before the meeting and it was carried.' This was an arrangement that endured little changed into the twenty-first century. It seems that the unusual origins of the Club, in a mixed whist club, had led to lady associate members briefly enjoying an equality of playing rights, but the Club quickly fell into line with other golf clubs and imposed playing restrictions on them.

The third issue was that of the Club's name. Newspaper reports show that the prefix Birkdale was soon added to give the title Birkdale Grosvenor Golf Club. Subsequently, there was correspondence from the Council of the Birkdale Golf Club concerning this name, and at the extraordinary general meeting held on the 5th December, it was announced that '…henceforth the Club would be known as the Southport Golf Club.' (See Fig.4) Having placated one of the two local senior clubs by dropping 'Birkdale' from the title, the feathers of the other were now ruffled. A member of the Hesketh Club wrote to the *Southport Visiter* welcoming the new club, but charging it with attempting to '…appropriate the history and reputation of the Southport Club', a club founded in 1885, which had recently been absorbed into the newly constituted Hesketh Golf Club. The Club did react and at a further Extraordinary General Meeting on 18th December the secretary reported that he had received notice of a motion to change the Club's name to the New Southport Golf Club. In the event the members present unanimously agreed that '…in deference to the wishes of the Hesketh Golf Club' the Club's name should be changed, but the name Southport and Ainsdale Golf Club was adopted. Why this name was chosen is something of a mystery: the entire proposed new course was within Birkdale, none of it was in Ainsdale, and it was several miles from the boundary with Southport. As Birkdale (which had absorbed Ainsdale in 1905) and Southport were separate local authorities, and very argumentative neighbours at that, it appears to be difficult to give a rational explanation for the choice other than the fact that it did not include 'Birkdale' and could hardly give offence to the Hesketh Club. What the new name did give was the potential for it to be reduced to the initials S&A, a title that would echo round the golfing world.

The infant Club was rapidly developing its traditions. The first Captain's Prize meeting, which was won by Walter Child, was held on 23rd March 1907. It was a thirty-six-hole event for the winners and the runners-up in monthly medals. In May, the last monthly medal played on the old course was played in two classes or divisions for the first time. The First Class was for players with a handicap of less than seventeen and the two divisions were pretty well balanced in size, with a few more competitors in the Second Class. It was about this time that the list of competitors for The Manchester Open, a regional competition for professionals and leading amateurs, included the name of E.A. Dixon (Southport and Ainsdale). Playing with a single figure handicap, he had a good record in Club events and appears to have been one of the first of many S&A members to carry the Club's name out into the wider world of golf. The golfing standard of the ladies appeared to be improving: the April ladies' medal was won by Miss Taylor, whose handicap was down to twenty and the runner-up had a handicap of twenty-five. It had become obvious that there was no immediate prospect of the railway company opening a station between Birkdale and Ainsdale, consequently it was decided to build a clubhouse on Liverpool Road about 200 yards south of the Crown Hotel. Planning permission was granted in May, and as a temporary measure the old wooden pavilion was moved to a site to the rear of the proposed clubhouse. An extension to provide dressing rooms and 'professional quarters' was added to the general club room. (See Fig. 18) The new course was opened for play on 14th May with a Whit mixed foursome competition. The Club had come a long way in the twelve months since its rather bizarre opening event.

Chapter Two
SOUTHPORT AND AINSDALE:
A NEW EIGHTEEN HOLE COURSE

*The Southport and Ainsdale Golf Club, which was originally established under
the Grosvenor Golf Club, have taken new ground which is now being laid out as
an eighteen hole golf course, and to place the finances of the present and new Club
on a satisfactory basis, in which every member, new or old, will have a financial
interest, it has been resolved to convert the Club into a Limited Liability Company.*
Circular Letter to Members, 1907

The official opening ceremony of the new course was held on the 15th June 1907. It included a programme of sports, competitions and an exhibition golf match between Anthony Spalding, a well-known amateur golfer and journalist from Manchester, and the Club's new professional, Hugh Roberts. Roberts was one of a succession of fine golfers who had learned their golf at Hoylake, and was described as being '…tall, lithe and a very good golfer with a free, easy style.' He came to S&A from Lucerne, Switzerland, where he had been working, and where George, one of his brothers, succeeded him. The day started fine and there was a large attendance of members and friends including Mr. C.J. Skitt, the agent of the Weld-Blundell Estate, who formally opened the course in the absence of the landowner. Although not a golfer he successfully hit an inaugural drive. Playing level, Roberts defeated Spalding 4 and 2 and the amateur was presented with a handsome gold medal to mark the occasion (Fig.8). Sadly, a downpour of rain curtailed other events, although Walter Sugg, who was a member of the organising committee, did win the driving competition. From the social point of view the opening was adjudged to be a great success. The facilities of the temporary pavilion were supplemented by the erection of a large marquee, in which afternoon tea was served, and what the *Southport Visiter* described as '…an excellent band was in attendance.'

In order to mark his contribution in helping to establish the Club, Mr. F.W. Smith had earlier been elected by the Board to be proposed as captain at the first Annual General Meeting. During this meeting, Walter Sugg's name was put forward as an alternative candidate, but the members decisively rejected this contentious amendment. Skitt, the landowner's agent who had arranged the lease for the course, was made an honorary member. A deputation unsuccessfully approached Charles Weld-Blundell, the landowner, to become president. He had earlier withdrawn from being the

F. W. Smith   A. T. Spalding   J. Linacre   H. Roberts   W. Sugg

8. Course opening ceremony 15th June 1907.
*This is a copy of a photograph, which appeared in the **Southport Visiter**.*

President of the Formby and Birkdale Golf Clubs and was distancing himself from direct contact with his Lancashire estates and spending much of his time in London, exercising his passion for the arts.

At the first Annual General Meeting a limit of 600 was placed on the number of members, of which a quarter could be ladies. The number of members was in fact 250, including eighty-two ladies or associates as they were classified. The pressure was on to increase the size of the membership and thus the income. To this end a large advertising hoarding inviting people to apply for membership was placed on the course facing the railway line. By the end on the year the overall membership had increased to just over 300, which included ten juvenile members. This category was restricted to youngsters who were in a member's family or lived with a member. John Linacre, who replaced Charles Leigh as secretary, gave a prize to be competed for by the juniors as early as 1907.

The expense associated with the new course and clubhouse led to financial difficulties and the debit on the current account rose to over a thousand pounds. 1908 did not see a significant growth in the number of members. Membership fees were the principal source from which the Board somewhat desperately sought to generate further income. First the joining fee was increased and when this strategy was deemed to have been counterproductive a reduction was tried. A scheme whereby members invited some 500 guests to play the course free of charge, in the hope that some of these visitors might subsequently apply for membership, was also introduced and quickly withdrawn. A new category of Conditional Member, with reduced playing rights, was introduced and the Club placed advertisements for new members in the local newspapers and the *Manchester Guardian*.

In 1909 the Board saw an opportunity to achieve a major boost in membership. Within a month of S&A's new course being opened the vacated nine-hole course at Dover Road was taken over by the Blundell Golf Club. This club had its origins in the Southport Athletic Golf Club, which had played on a small course at Blowick. A club for working-class men, it was founded by W.A. Findlay, a Scottish doctor and local politician. He personally rented the Dover Road course and formed the Blundell Club to provide golf without '…burdening the members with the heavy expenses usually associated with the game.' The joining fee was a fifth of that for S&A. Inheriting an established if primitive course and thus facing only low overheads, Findlay's concept proved successful. Indeed, taking in several additional fields extended the course, allowing some of the nine holes to be lengthened. The Blundell Club was judged to be '…in an exceedingly prosperous condition' when, in 1909, the financially stretched Southport and Ainsdale Club approached it with a view to amalgamation. The longer lease that S&A had secured from the Estate was an attractive lure, but, after lengthy negotiations, a majority of the Blundell members rejected the proposition. Their annual subscription was only half of that at S&A.

Golf Clubs in Southport: Fees c.1910

	Entrance	Annual	Green
Hesketh	£10.50	£2.62	£0.12
Birkdale	£10.50	£2.62	£0.12
Southport and Ainsdale	£ 5.25	£2.10	£0.10
Blundell	£ 1.05	£1.05	£0.05

Source: *Lancashire and Yorkshire Railway: Where to Golf*

Some members of the Blundell Club unsuccessfully approached S&A about the possibility of joining as individuals, with some remission of the entrance fee. Later, in 1911, the Estate re-located the Blundell Club on what was to become an attractive nine-hole course to the south of Ainsdale village.

Another initiative to raise money was through the many hotels and hydropathic establishments in Southport. The hotels were supplied with advertising material and acted as agents, receiving twenty per cent commission for selling temporary membership tickets for S&A to their visitors.

A novel open amateur competition was introduced in 1910, partially as a vehicle to generate additional green fee income (Fig.9). A prize of a fifty ounce silver cup was offered and competitors could submit as many cards as they wished in a qualifying round that had to be played between April and July. The players who had submitted the best sixteen scores then went on to match play, on occasions fixed by them, with dates having been specified by the Club for the completion of each round.

The land for the new course consisted of approximately 100 acres. The railway again provided the western boundary; the inland boundary was dictated by development along Liverpool Road South; a spur containing two holes extended as far north as Balshaw's Farm, close to Sandon Road, whilst the southern boundary was at the Birkdale Cemetery. (See front endpaper) George Lowe, the architect, was the professional at Lytham, having previously been an assistant to Tom Morris at St Andrews and Jack Morris at Royal Liverpool. Never an outstanding golfer, his major reputation was as a club maker but he was also a leading golf architect and was responsible for designing over 120 courses, including the new course at Lytham (Fig.10). At S&A he followed the common practice of the day, accepting the existing topography, utilising available hazards, and thus keeping construction costs down to a minimum.

The length of the course was just short of 6,000 yards and the bogey was 77. The land was not uniformly dune heath and as a result the eighteen-hole course had two distinct and different nines. Nine holes were on relatively flat land, much of which had previously been under cultivation (Fig.11). Cops again featured as hazards on these holes. The golf correspondent of the *Manchester Courier* described a cop on the 5th hole as 'decidedly quaint' and judged it to be unfair. It was a hole of about 260 yards, and some ten to fifteen yards short of the green there was a low grassy cop about a foot

WEIGHT
50 oz.
SILVER.

VALUE:
FIFTEEN
GUINEAS.

TO BE WON OUTRIGHT IN

Open Amateur Competition.

The SOUTHPORT & AINSDALE GOLF CLUB

Offer the above prize to be competed for during the Summer of 1910,
under the following conditions:

9. Section of a poster for an Open Amateur Competition 1910.

*10. George Lowe driving on the 2nd tee at Lytham c.1888. The field cop in the
background was a 'hazard' in front of the 1st green.*

high running across the line. He complained that a fine drive could be '...tucked up under the hazard', thus preventing a run-up shot and a possible three. Field cops were progressively removed from the course; whilst bunkers and 'sand scrapes' were created. There were also some natural bunkers. The most famous hazard was a huge bunker - 'The Grave' - in front of the green on the 18th 'Home' hole. Its deep face was revetted, and part of its walls was constructed with railway sleepers (Fig.12). The *Southport Visiter* correspondent wrote that: 'All the greens are well guarded by natural hazards, a foozle meeting its just deserts.' (A 'foozle' was a mishit shot. The word was also used as a verb and appears quite frequently in the writings of P.G. Wodehouse.) The rest of the course, including the southern portion, was described as being '...sporty hilly country.' One commentator wrote that the links had been '...created out of a veritable wilderness.'

A ridge of tall sandhills, level with Birkdale Cemetery, marked the southern boundary of the course. This ridge still runs across the 3rd and 16th holes and continues into the Hillside course, behind its 2nd green. This feature, which was taller in 1907, was to give S&A its signature hole. Walter Child wrote: 'We were faced with a formidable sandhill if we were ever to make any use whatever of a very bad bit of land at the extreme boundary to the south of our leased land.' Child favoured clearing a complete opening in the ridge to enable a player to see where he was going. Hobart Gumbley, a fellow director and a fourteen-handicap golfer, wanted only a part of the sandhill cleared and the building of a bunker in its face (Fig.13). Sidney Murphy, another Board member and one of the Club's leading golfers, backed Gumbley and the famous feature that was to take his name was

11. An extraordinary panoramic photograph of the northern end of the course c.1910.

Electricity Sub-Station   **Lloyd's Sidings**   **Hill Side Farm**   **Sando Road**

created. Just over the bunker the land fell to the green, at the back of which was the field cop, which marked the course boundary (Fig.14). This 7th hole was a bogey five and apparently when Gumbley played it for the first time he took fourteen strokes. Later, for a short period of time, the hole was shortened and played as a bogey three. The sleepers, which cost one shilling (5p) each from the Cheshire Lines Railway, were added to the face of the bunker in 1911. This hazard, visible from the railway, rapidly became notorious and Ernest Whitcombe, one of three brothers who played in the 1935 Ryder Cup was to describe Gumbley's as 'the finest hole in England'.

Child's rejected scheme for the 7th was an effort to avoid a blind shot to the green. He later wrote that: 'The curse of our new course was that every hole had either a blind drive, or worse still a very bad blind approach to the green.' This was to be a recurring criticism of this course. A further complaint was that hidden ditches threatened some drives. It was suggested that these '…inhibited the golfer and encouraged him to play an iron from the tee and thus be left with a long wood shot to the green.' As a result of these complaints several ditches were culverted.

Within a few months of the course being opened, minor amendments were being made to its boundaries and the layout was anything but settled. Small parcels of land were lost, whilst others were gained and new holes created. Annual reports regularly reported that the Green Committee had 'improved and extended the course'. By 1913 two new holes were created on land which had been leased behind Birkdale Cemetery, south of the original course boundary. The tee for a new 8th hole, which ran south-west

'The Grave'
18th Hole

Crown Hotel

Liverpool Road

*12. Hugh Roberts, the professional, playing from 'The Grave', which was the
biggest local bunker. Liverpool Road and the Crown Hotel are in the background.*

13. The sleeper-faced bunker guarding Gumbley's green c.1913.

*14. Gumbley's green at the southern extremity of the course c.1908.
The boundary is marked by a fence, cop and ditch on the left.*

*15. Players putting out on Gumbley's green c.1912. The field cop behind this green was part of the original
course boundary. The new 8th tee can be seen in the left foreground and the new fenced 9th green on the right.*

alongside the railway, was to the right of Gumbley's green and the new green was that of the present 17th hole. Returning towards Gumbley's, the tee for the new 9th hole was at the side of the present 2nd fairway, where the site can still be seen, and the green was close to the then Gumbley's green (Fig.15).

It is interesting to note that in 1912 the Local Rules included eight references to cops, which formed part of the boundaries of the course. Much of the land abutting on to the golf course was still being farmed, and a local rule stated that a player recovering a ball from a field in which crops were growing, would be disqualified or suffer a loss of hole. The secretary wrote to the farmers requesting that all the balls found should be returned to the professional for reselling to members. Surprisingly, perhaps, cows were still allowed to graze the course and the greens were still fenced. A local rule allowed that: 'A ball laying in dung may be lifted and dropped without loss or penalty.' There was increasing concern about the condition of the fairways. A notice in the clubhouse asked members to inform the secretary if any member failed to replace a divot, so that disciplinary action could be taken.

It was not only golfers who were inflicting damage to the course. It appears that rabbits were also active. It seems that it was the 18th hole that suffered worst and the Board paid a local farmer to attempt to control their numbers. Later the Club let the shooting and trapping rights. The rabbits must have been unpopular with the members as relief from a rabbit hole or scrape cost a shot.

Green Committee minutes reveal that the tees had mats on them and alongside them were salt-glazed earthenware pots, from which the players took a handful of sand to create a tee for the ball. On the 1st tee was a wooden device called a 'ball starter', used to manage starting. (See Fig.22) On several holes there were marker posts to indicate the location of the green. Black-painted bamboo poles, topped with flags made from yellow cloth were in the holes.

Although critical of the layout, most commentators were generous in their judgements about the condition of the course. A pony-drawn mower had been purchased in 1908. The land was well drained and the course rarely had to be closed because of standing water, a problem that had plagued the nearby Birkdale course in its early years. A number of wells were dug to provide irrigation. Wooden barrels were bought to line these wells. Regular minor changes to the course continued. New holes were formed and others modified. Although criticism of the course, in the golfing press, continued, it was generally agreed that S&A was on golfing country of great potential but that the Club needed to take advice from one of the leading golf course designers, if the promise was to be realised.

Hugh Roberts, the professional, was paid a wage of one pound a week and he was allowed to charge one and sixpence (7.5p) for a one-hour lesson. Sadly, he suffered a serious illness and died in August 1908. His brother Percy, a golfer of similar style who had been deputising for him, became the professional and was to serve the Club for some forty years. The early years of the Club were in the era of full-time boy caddies. Board minutes show that it attempted to regulate and improve the provision of caddies, a role undertaken by the professional. An attempt to introduce a rule stating that: 'Players with caddies have a priority over players without caddies' was resisted. The boys were allowed limited opportunities to play on the course and competitions were held for them, but by 1911, Winston Churchill, the Home Secretary, was nationally advocating the employment of elderly unemployed men as caddies in order to prevent boys entering this 'blind alley' occupation. Significantly the S&A Board discussed the question of insurance for caddies in 1912 but it was to be new National Insurance Regulations, which required contributions to be paid for insurance stamps, that brought an end to the full-time employment of boys as caddies. When the Lancashire County Championship was played at S&A in 1914, the Club employed a retired policeman as a temporary caddiemaster for the three days of the meeting. It seems that he was short of caddies and that he met boys outside St. John's School in Sandon Road and 'enticed' twelve of them to miss school and go to S&A to act as caddies. As a result the Club received a letter from the Town Clerk, which threatened legal action. Another warning about boys serving as caddies was received in 1921, and the Board instructed the professional that the '…regulations must be adhered to.'

Local boys consistently trespassed on the course, sometimes searching for lost balls. In 1913 a nine-year-old and a twelve-year-old appeared in court accused of stealing fifteen balls, which they had found on S&A and then sold. Both were sentenced to six strokes of the birch. A more lenient view was taken of another boy who vandalised a wooden tee box and was fined one shilling (5p).

The site for the clubhouse was on Liverpool Road about 200 yards south of the Crown Hotel. It was claimed that '…access from both the high road and railway is somewhat unique.' In fact Birkdale Station was something approaching a mile and half distant, whilst the tram terminus was at the

Crown Hotel (Fig.16). Trams ran every fifteen minutes. The expectation that: 'By a little coaxing the tramway terminus may be extended to the clubhouse' was not to be fulfilled. It was hoped that selling five-pound income-yielding debenture shares, for which the clubhouse would provide '...ample security', would raise the £1500 needed to build and furnish it. Despite a number of direct appeals, members were reluctant to purchase these shares. In addition, a high proportion of the five-pound Preference (privilege) Shares also remained unsold. H. Halsall, an Ainsdale architect won a 'sealed competition' to design the clubhouse '...with a view to be adapted as a pair of villas at some, to be hoped, very distant time.' This requirement was recognition that landowners only gave golf clubs short leases and were ready to surrender parts of a course to demands from builders. In fact the lease for the clubhouse was for ninety-nine years, much longer than that of twenty-one which had been given for the course.

The clubhouse was opened in August 1908 (Fig.17a&b). It had '...a capacious first-floor dining room facing the links', there was a small balcony and in 1912 a member donated a large clock. A small putting green was created behind the clubhouse. For a brief period the Club employed a uniformed pageboy, whilst in the lounge members were able to read *Punch, The Tatler, Sporting and Dramatic Illustrated* and *Golf Illustrated.* Clubhouse facilities also included a card room, a smoke room and a ladies' lounge. At the Annual General Meeting in May 1909 the members were informed that:

16. *The tram terminus at the Crown Hotel. The Crown, formerly a small country pub, had long served the Birkdale farming community, but urban expansion in this area had prompted its re-building and enlargement in 1898.*

17. The Liverpool Road clubhouse c.1910.
(a) The east front overlooking the road. (b) The west front overlooking the course.

> While no doubt of benefit to the members, it has caused a great increase in working expenses without any immediate benefits. Share capital not having been taken up as expected, the Directors have had to obtain an overdraft from the bank to pay for the clubhouse.

An extension to the lounge was proposed as early as 1909 but it was 1914 before this addition was completed at a cost of £200 (Fig. 18). The ladies unsuccessfully approached the Board to have their lounge extended out to the same level. Further improvements to the building in the form of a new locker room, new lavatories, and a shed for members' bicycles were undertaken without having to increase the overdraft. A cycle shed was a necessary amenity for a golf club at this time. It was only in 1914 that the Club designated a small area of land, surrounded by a post and chain fence, to be used as a car park.

In 1910 the Club was faced with negotiation with the Weld-Blundell Estate about the future of the course. The Estate wanted to offer a new lease involving an exchange of land. The possibility of a railway station, close to the electricity powerhouse, was looming larger and Weld-Blundell wanted residential development on what was the northern part of the links. A sub-committee of the Board was formed to consider the problem. They assumed that the building of a railway station would result in a surge in membership from people living along the 'line'. Their recommendations involved accepting new land to replace the lost acreage. Although the clubhouse would thus be cut off from the course it seems that the Estate would permit the retention of an isthmus of land that would allow access. In fact the station failed to materialize and a new twenty-one year lease, for the existing course, was signed in 1912. The Board's proposal had also included the acquisition of a further fifty acres to build a separate eighteen-hole ladies' course. This scheme was overtaken by the signing of the new lease, when it was put on the back burner and it was then lost during the Great War.

An odd threat to the future of the Club occurred in December 1912. The Lancashire and Yorkshire Railway Company served a Parliamentary Notice on the Club informing it that it intended to run a new branch line from Kew Station, on Scarisbrick New Road in Southport, round the inland boundary of the borough to Ainsdale. Plans were posted in the clubhouse showing how this proposed development ran across the links, past Windy Harbour Farm. Arbitrators were appointed, and it was only when the Bill was

18. The clubhouse with the extended lounge c.1920.
The golfers are approaching the professional's shop, formerly the temporary clubhouse.

approaching its Royal Assent that the Company decided to withdraw the scheme, which would almost certainly have left it with a white elephant, and the Club possibly seeking a new course.

An S&A membership book for 1912 lists 282 male members, without showing to which categories they belonged. Approximately a quarter of them lived outside the borough: forty-six members lived along the railway line to Liverpool, sixteen on the line to Manchester, and ten outside Lancashire. 116 of the members lived in Southport; the numbers living in Scarisbrick New Road (nine), Hampton Road (nine), Lord Street (nine), and Forest Road (six) are indicative of their distribution. Of the seventy-nine members living in Birkdale, twelve lived in the socially superior Birkdale Park, on the other side of the line. The majority of the remainder lived on Liverpool Road or in the side roads running from it. Only fifteen of the members lived in Ainsdale, and twelve of these came from the new residential development of Ainsdale-on-Sea. The membership included at least nine doctors, whilst accountants, solicitors, surveyors, bank managers, a clergyman and the headmaster of the Southport School of Art represented other professions. Occupations such as merchants, brokers, agents, and travellers were indications of the world of commerce. There did not appear to be many manufacturers, although Nettleton of 'Nettleton & Wooley', a local mineral water manufacturer, was included. The list included many other names whose family businesses prospered in Southport: Giddens the photographer, who was responsible for many of the early photographs of the course, Hindle the estate agent, Bamber the motor-car dealer, Calvert the jeweller, Ayris the furrier, Hiscocks the Birkdale provision merchant, and Aldridges the musical instrument shop. Locally born William Rimmer, the nationally renowned brass band conductor and composer, was also a member. He presented the Club with 500 copies of his *Golf Song* (A copy of which survives in the archives). It seems that S&A acquired its reputation for musical entertainment early in its life. S&A was undoubtedly a successful middle-class club, but without the social exclusiveness of its longer established neighbours.

There were 145 lady members, fifty-eight of whom were wives or daughters of male members. It seems that from the earliest days the S&A ladies' section attracted and accepted an unusually high proportion of its number from outside the circle of family membership. Daughters of members accounted for less than a quarter of the eighty-three 'Misses' listed. The proportion of ladies living within the borough was much higher than was the case for the men; only six lived outside Southport and they were all either the wives or daughters of members. Three, two of whom were in one family, lived along the Liverpool 'line', whilst the other three lived in distant places and included one who lived with her husband in Calcutta.

The ladies' section was active during this period. From 1907 the Board had sanctioned the election of a ladies' committee and a lady captain, not a common occurrence in this era. The first lady captain was Mrs. F.W. Smith, the wife of the Club's first captain. It seems, however, that the relationship between the Board and the ladies was not all sweetness and light. The question of the degree of autonomy that was allowed to the Ladies' Committee was a major issue. The Board insisted that the ladies were not empowered to make any decisions until the Board had approved their committee's recommendations. The question of playing rights continued to be contentious, and, in the years that followed, the Board consistently attempted to restrict lady associate status to members' family.

There was a growing programme of domestic competitions for the ladies, but prior to handicaps becoming subject to external supervision there were problems. One competition 'winner' had to surrender her prize; whilst following an incident in another competition a lady refused to accept a ruling from the Board and engaged a solicitor. Having taken what the Board described as '...vexatious legal proceedings' she was asked to resign, but later, following an apology, she was allowed to retain her membership. Miss L. Taylor continued to be the Club's dominant lady golfer. She won the Captain's Prize in four consecutive years from 1907, again on the first occasion it was contested after the war in 1920, and finally in 1924. A second major trophy, the Coronation Challenge Cup was donated to the ladies by Mrs. H. Hall in 1911, and later became known as the Hall Cup. Miss Taylor won it in 1915. She also served as lady captain in 1913, and did a stint as honorary secretary in the 1920s, before resigning when she got married in 1924. The ladies' golfing calendar also included driving and pitching competitions, both played as the best of three attempts on designated holes. By 1910 there was a fixture with Preston Golf Club and, in 1912 a match against the Formby Ladies' Club was played. The Board had earlier ruled that the Club would not pay for the entertaining of visiting teams. In 1912 the Club joined the Ladies' Golf Union, and in the following year the Lancashire Ladies' County Golf Association staged a county match against Cheshire, the reigning county champions, at S&A.

The Board exercised close supervision of the ladies' section. In 1912 the secretary was instructed to inform the Ladies' Committee that the '...noisy character of conversation in the dining room' was unacceptable, a reprimand that was repeated a month later. In the following year all the lady associates received a printed post card from the ladies' secretary telling them that '...following representations to the Board concerning congestion on the course...in a summer evening' the ladies were requested to allow men players to go through.

The Club had developed a strong programme of men's annual competitions. Trophies included the Dyson Mallinson Shield, which was donated in 1907, last contested in 1924, and can still be seen in the clubhouse. Hobart Gumbley won this shield in 1908, and other winners included six captains of the Club. The first winner of the Blackburn-Holden Cup was Walter Child in 1910. An early holder of the amateur course record was Walter Sugg who scored 75 against the bogey of 77 in 1908. He also won the Captain's Prize in that year. Sidney Murphy, who followed Smith as Captain, won this prize in the following two years and established a new course record. In addition there were numerous prizes to be won outright, the principal one being at Easter, when a knockout competition was played over the holiday weekend. Walter Sugg, one of the Club's most accomplished golfers and a member of the Board serving on the Finance, Handicap, Green and Building Committees, became involved in a dispute arising in a match, ironically in a competition for a cup he had presented. (In the previous year, he had also presented a gold medal as a prize for an aggregate competition.) Refusing to accept the Board's ruling, Sugg referred the matter to the St Andrews Rules of Golf Committee and retained a solicitor. His fellow directors suggested that in the light of his conduct he ought to resign his seat on the Board. At this juncture he accepted the ruling and continued to serve on the Board until his resignation from the Club in 1912. Sugg was undoubtedly a major figure, both on and off the course, in the early years of S&A. F.W. Smith described him as having played an important role in the Club's foundation, although it was Sugg who had contested his election as captain in 1907. Sugg was one of the two directors to sign the early share certificates. (See Fig.7) He did rejoin in 1919 but left two years later. Significantly his name does not appear at all in Child's account of the infant club. He obviously decided that this controversial figure should be airbrushed out of the Club's history.

Southport and Ainsdale demonstrated that it was an outward looking club. As early as 1910, the Club invited local professionals to hold a prize meeting on the course and contributed a guinea (£1.05) to the prize fund. Later in that year two visiting professionals overstepped the limits of acceptable behaviour, when, after playing the course, they '...used the clubhouse without authority'. The secretary was instructed to '...prevent a recurrence of such transgression.' In April 1912 the Northern Section of the Professional Golfers' Association played its then prestigious Leeds Challenge Cup competition at S&A. Few professional golfers played outside their home region at that time. Peter McEwan, the Hesketh professional, who set a course record of 78, won the cup. Adverse criticism of the wooden post and wire fences, which surrounded each green, led to them being temporarily removed for this event. The *Liverpool Courier* golf correspondent's report of the competition, which included severe criticism of the impression created by these fences normally present at S&A, probably contributed to their permanent removal.

The infant club was seeking to establish links with other clubs in the area. Early opponents in matches were the YMCA and the Banking and Insurance clubs. In the absence of opportunity to play with the more established clubs in the locality, S&A looked further afield and fixtures with the Preston, West Cheshire and Prenton clubs were accepted. In 1921 the captains of the Hesketh and Banking and Insurance golf clubs were guests at S&A's annual dinner. The following year the captains of Birkdale, Ormskirk, Huyton and Preston were also invited.

S&A joined the Lancashire Union of Golf Clubs in 1910 and one of the members – R.G. Boulden - was soon to serve as its honorary assistant secretary. Three S&A men took part in the inaugural Lancashire County Championship in 1910. They were Sidney Murphy whose handicap was plus two, Walter Sugg (four) and Hobart Gumbley (ten). The Club volunteered to stage the Union's annual championship in 1914, and the county executive, '…being aware of the improvements on the course and in the clubhouse', accepted the offer. On the first day, the thirty-six-hole qualifying event for the Rayner Batty Trophy was interrupted by a violent thunderstorm and reduced to eighteen holes. The result of the subsequent knock-out tournament was deemed to be: '…a very big surprise to everyone.' A little-known tradesman, Sam Robinson, who was a member of the modest Southport YMCA Golf Club, won the championship.

Sam Robinson later joined S&A and became the Club's first golfing giant, that is, one who made a significant impact in the wider world of national and international golf. He was in many ways an unusual hero. At a time when class barriers were much more a part of everyday life than is the case today, the presence of a working-class tradesman as a member of a leading golf club was an unusual event in itself. He was, however, an outstanding golfer, whose S&A handicap of plus six made him one of the highest ranked amateur golfers in the country. Born in High Park, Southport, he had acted as a part-time caddie on the links of the Southport (later Hesketh) Golf Club, whilst still a schoolboy. At that time the club played on the Moss Lane course close to his home. Being a caddie was a full-time occupation for many local school leavers, and, at the age of fourteen, Sam temporarily followed this path. It was whilst he was a caddie that he learned to swing a club. He later claimed that G.F. Smith, Hesketh's great international and champion golfer, had inspired him. As at S&A, members encouraged the young caddies to play the game and occasional tournaments were arranged for them. Apart from the advice and help he received at this time he never had any serious tuition. Indeed, between the ages of fifteen and twenty-one it seems that Sam had nothing to do with golf. In 1909 he emigrated to Canada, where he stayed with relatives, returning to Southport two years later.

In the year of his departure to Canada the Moss Lane course was brought back into service by the Southport YMCA, and it was as a member of this club that Sam got his club handicap down to plus seven, in two years. This was an extraordinary achievement and testimony to his natural ability and flair. 'He trained by playing round after round against the best-ball of three single figure handicap men.' He had two brothers who were also talented

Tolley's Conqueror.

19. Sam Robinson
English Amateur Championship 1925.

golfers, one was to reach the semi-final of the county championship. It was, however, on the S&A course that Sam was to '...emerge from relative obscurity and win the Lancashire Championship' in 1914. Sam was a working plumber and as such his success in this middle-class sport attracted much publicity. The *Liverpool Courier* headline read simply: 'The Artisan Golfer'. He told Anthony Spalding, the *Manchester Guardian* golf correspondent that he entered the Lancashire Championship because he recognised that success would help him to fulfil his ambition to become a golf professional.

After deciding to remain an amateur, Sam joined S&A in 1919, as a thirty-one-year-old, and embarked on a new stage in the golfing career that was to bring him and the Club many honours. In 1925 he was the defeated finalist in the inaugural English Amateur Championship, which was played at Hoylake. After eliminating the favourite, Cyril Tolley, in an earlier round, he lost to a member of the home Royal Liverpool Club in the thirty-six-hole final (Fig.19). In the five years between 1925 and 1929 he won the Lancashire Championship four times. His record of being champion on five occasions was finally equalled in 2005. Qualification for this event was over thirty-six holes and he led the field to win the Rayner Batty trophy on six occasions. S&A marked his achievement of reaching the final of the English Amateur Championship and winning the Lancashire Championship in 1925 with a celebration dinner, at which Sam was made an honorary life member. His 'golfing friends' presented him with a case of cutlery and a gold watch. He first played for the County in 1920 and went on to play twenty-six times. Opportunities to play international golf were limited in those days, but he was an English International in six consecutive years from

1925 to 1930, when he would have been forty-two. In 1926 Sam was passed over when the British team was selected to meet the Americans in the Walker Cup, an omission that caused the Lancashire Union sufficient concern for it to be officially discussed at a committee meeting. In 1924 he qualified to play in the Open Championship at Royal Liverpool, beating Walter Hagen's qualifying score at Formby. Hagen went on to win the championship.

A regular competitor in Club events Sam compiled an unequalled record of success. He won the Blackburn Holden Cup twice, the Championship Trophy a record fourteen times, the Easter Match Play Championship six times, and the Captain's Prize five times, the last occasion being in 1950, when he was sixty-two. Playing around his home course, he regularly achieved sensationally low scores. In June 1922, whilst playing in a friendly four-ball, with three former captains of the Club, all of whom signed his card, Sam scored 68, which was ten under bogey (Fig.20). Sam took a full role in the life of the Club and within a year of becoming a member he was serving on the Green Committee.

Invitations for him to play in exhibition and charity matches were frequent. One such match, in 1926 at S&A, involved the American Walter Hagen. (See Fig.31) Hagen described him as the best amateur he had ever seen and was so impressed by Sam's ability that he invited him to accompany him to the United States with a view to playing professionally. Although Hagen promised to make Sam's fortune, he declined to go. Crewe Roden, the Club Secretary and a former captain, told a tale of a more informal match at S&A. It seems that a visitor from Manchester was looking for a game and Roden approached Sam, who

20. Sam Robinson - 'Ten under bogey' 1922.

was in the clubhouse, to ask whether he would be willing to make up. Sam agreed and after introductions, the visitor, who was later to settle in the town and become an S&A captain, politely informed Sam that his handicap was scratch. Sam with the usual twinkle in his eye replied in his broad local dialect 'That's awreet, lad, I'll gi thee four shots.' Self-deprecation was the basis of much of his humour. When he was selected to play in his first Lancashire county match in 1920, he was approached by a fellow team member and asked if he would like a lift by car. After accepting the offer, Sam was then asked if he was on the telephone. In answer Sam replied 'Telephone? We've not even got Company watta.' (Many local residents had not signed up to be connected to the piped water supply, opting instead to rely on the free ground water, drawn through the cast iron pump which invariably sat alongside the slopstone in working-class Southport kitchens.) As well as enjoying a lively sense of humour, it appears that this considerable competitor was a '...frank outspoken man'.

Testimonies to his golfing achievements are many, although praise of his golfing style is rare (Fig.21). 'There are those who would

21. Sam Robinson -
S&A's first golfing great c.1926.

say that Sam Robinson was a very good golfer in spite of his swing, but particularly, in spite of his weak left hand grip.' 'Every shot he played was cut and brought in from the left.' Consequently '...his length from the tee was only average, however, his accuracy was remarkable and his short game was superb, added to this he was an incredible accurate putter.' The approach was his favourite shot. V.A.S. Beanland, the *Liverpool Daily Post* golf correspondent, wrote that his putting style was reminiscent of Harold Hilton the great Hoylake Open Champion. 'He grasps the putter half way down the shaft, and bending almost double, strikes a beautifully true ball.' On occasions when this style let him down he would go to the opposite extreme '...holding his putter at the top of the grip and standing nearly upright.'

He was also described as 'a thoughtful golfer'. The *Manchester Guardian* golf correspondent, describing his play in the 1914 County Championship, wrote that:

> …one of the most striking features of his play was the perfect manner in which he used wooden clubs through the green. Other players seemed to find it difficult to lift the ball with a brassy, and often took turf in doing it, but Robinson appeared hardly to touch the ground and yet the ball went into the air. His confidence was so great that sometimes he used a driver for his second shot.

A tale which points to the precision of Sam's ball striking concerned a fellow competitor who marvelled at his ability to control the height of his ball in a strong wind. It seems that he could consistently hit the ball low into the wind and high down wind. His explanation was simple, into the wind he hit the ball with the lower part of the shallow clubface, whilst down wind he used the upper part. S&A might not have had a practice ground at this time, but, at home, Sam had fastened a bed mattress against a wall in order to provide a primitive indoor driving range. He fitted up a similar facility at the gas showrooms, where he worked; whilst at home he built a covered practice tee in his back garden, from which he could hit balls onto the adjoining Old Links (formerly the YMCA) course, when it was deserted in bad weather.

Sam did not share the social background of most of his golfing contemporaries. This helped to make him newsworthy, attracting headlines in regional and national, as well as local newspapers. He continued to live in High Park and worked as an assistant in the Corporation gas showroom. It seems that the authority appreciated the public relations value of employing such a distinguished amateur golfer. Nevertheless, opportunities to fully participate in the amateur golf circuit were denied by his economic circumstances and no doubt by social barriers within the golfing world. It is tempting to speculate on just what Sam might have achieved in different circumstances.

World War One was to have a great impact on the Club. A Japanese Oak memorial recorded the fact that six of the forty-two members who served in the armed forces, made the supreme sacrifice in this bloody conflict. Members in the armed forces were made honorary members for the duration of their service, whilst golfers serving locally were offered the courtesy of the course. The clubhouse was closed earlier in the evening, and wartime shortages contributed to a decline in social activity. There were no inter-club matches in 1915. The Club's income was dramatically reduced and these were financially difficult years. The Board reported that it had '…taken all possible steps towards economy and reduction in expenditure.'

Levies were placed on members in an attempt to balance the books. An annual sum of two pounds was later replaced by threepence (1.25p) a round. The Estate helped by deferring the rent and allowing it to be paid in modest monthly instalments. To save money, some members painted the pavilion in 1917. As much of the course was on former agricultural land, the Club was required to plough up the 4th and 5th fairways, adjacent to Peter Lloyd's Hill Side Farm, for vegetable production. Eight tons of manure were bought in order to fertilize this ground for growing potatoes. Growing hay on the course was an obvious and simple response to the demands of the War Agricultural Committee. Initially, members volunteered to do the haymaking and the hay was sold at five pounds per ton. Later the Club raised seventy-five pounds per annum by leasing the grazing and mowing rights.

In 1917 the Club successfully hosted an exhibition match held in aid of local hospital war charities. The participants included two of golf's so-called 'Great Triumvirate'. They were James Braid and John Taylor, both five times winners of the Open Championship. The third, and absent, member was Harry Vardon, who had won the Open a record six times. The four ball at S&A was made up by Ted Ray, the winner of the 1912 Open Championship, who would go on to win the U.S. Open in 1920, and T.G. Renouf, a well-known professional from Hopwood, Manchester (Fig.22). On other occasions, wounded servicemen from some of the town's many military hospitals were entertained for lunch at the Club, followed by a musical concert provided by members (Fig.23).

In 1918, Western Command wanted to lease nine acres of the course, adjacent to Windy Harbour Road, for use as an internment camp. The Club was to receive an annual rent of thirty-five pounds and the authorities would pay for the fairway and green to be restored after occupation. Preparations were started but the scheme was abandoned and the Club received compensation for the damage caused. The end of hostilities came later in that year, and the institution of two new annual competitions marked the return of members from active service. Members donated generously to commission an original work of art in bronze, which became the Peace Trophy. This moving bronze is of a private soldier of the local Kings Liverpool Regiment. (Three of the six members who lost their lives served with this regiment.) The infantryman is without a rifle and in the act of discarding his webbing, thus symbolising the end of hostilities (Fig.24). It is a unique artefact as the Club refused the artists' request to have further castings made. Initially, participation in the Peace Trophy was restricted to members who had served in the forces during the war. Another competition

22. A wartime exhibition match for charity 1917.
The four players holding clubs are: J.H.Taylor, Ted Ray, James Braid and T.G. Renouf.

23. A group of wounded soldiers in front of the extended lounge.

24. The Peace Trophy. This unique trophy was executed by local artists Mr. and Mrs. G.J. Mitchell.

introduced during this period was the St. Dunstan's, with the proceeds going to the National Institution for the Blind, in recognition of its work for injured servicemen.

The immediate post-war years saw a continuation of economically hard times for the Club. 'The successful operation of the levy' on members in 1919, brought some relief. The Club also wrote to the holders of Preference Shares, suggesting that it could no longer afford the associated privileges. Following a meeting, the majority of this group agreed to augment their subscriptions by contributing a donation. The accounts for the following year showed a return to profitability, being in the black to the tune of £184.

It was at this juncture in its history that the Club faced its most dramatic crisis to date. Under an Act of Parliament, the Southport Corporation served the Club with notice that it intended to build a new arterial road through the course. This would extend Waterloo Road over a new railway bridge, to link with Liverpool Road about 300 yards south of the clubhouse. The Corporation was able to make the necessary compulsory purchase of land under the Unemployed (Relief Works) Act of 1920. The extension would bring obvious improvements to Southport's link with Ainsdale, but it was principally part of a national scheme designed to help alleviate the extensive unemployment that the post-war economic depression had inflicted on the country (Fig.25). This initiative appears to have taken the Club by surprise, its first mention in the Board minutes is in October 1921, up to this point the Board appears to have been anticipating the continued occupation and upgrading of the Liverpool Road clubhouse.

Planned to run across the 1st and 18th fairways, the road would completely isolate the clubhouse from the bulk of the course. (See rear endpaper) Further land would be required alongside the road for residential development, and the Corporation wanted an additional twelve and a half acres for the site for a school – now Birkdale High School. The consequence would be the loss of six of the existing holes. Only a radical solution would provide an eighteen-hole course with a conveniently sited clubhouse. Following a meeting of the members, the Board was authorised to carry out and complete the necessary negotiations with the landowners, the

25. Waterloo Road extension c.1926.
In the background the new railway bridge for Hillside Station. (See map, rear endpaper.)

Weld-Blundell Estate, the Corporation and the Railway Company, in the best interests of the Club. All the surrounding land was considered in the search for an alternative site, including looking at possibilities to the north of the existing clubhouse, and on the seaward side of the railway line, land later occupied by the Hillside Club. The possibility of having all eighteen holes to the west of the railway was considered, as was that of having holes on both sides of the track. There was a precedent for such a layout at West Lancashire, where a footbridge linked the two portions of the course. It soon became evident, however, that the best option was to be found by extending the course south towards Ainsdale, thus adding to the twelve holes that would survive. A basic agreement was quickly reached, but settling unresolved details meant that the negotiations dragged on until 1924, long after much of the initial construction work had been completed.

A new twenty-one year lease was granted for the course and James Braid, not only a great golfer, but also one of the country's most successful and sought after golf architects, was commissioned to design the six new holes at the Ainsdale end, re-model the others and '...secure links of championship

41

quality.' He was asked to use existing greens as far as was practicable. (See Fig.48) His new holes were the 1st, 2nd, 6th, 7th, 8th and 18th. One of the bonuses of the change was that the six holes that had been lost had been on the dullest, flattest part of the course. In return the Club received what Walter Child described as 'jungle country', but this was land, which would shape into S&A's magnificent links (Fig.26). Henry Cotton later described Braid as having '…a great eye for a golf hole.' He claimed that he could '…cross a tract of virgin land and plan out golf holes as well as any man.' The 2nd green, built into the side of one of the great dunes provides an example of Braid's 'vision'. Professional Jack McLachlan later described it as being of '…an armchair type, with the arm to the right missing', a steep slope leading up to the green tends to turn the approach off to that side. Guy Farrar, an outstanding golfer and journalist, suggested that spectators standing on the tall sandhill behind this green '…would feel like Gods on Olympus watching the battles of the heroes below.' A similar elevated green is found on the 8th hole.

The new course measured 6,350 yards, not a '…paradise for the mere slugger'. V.A.S. Beanland wrote:

> The course will be sufficiently severe to test the low handicap man without breaking the hearts of the 'Rabbits', if they emerged so far from the rabbit stage as to be fairly certain of getting their drives away. For at Southport and Ainsdale there is small mercy for the 'foozler' from the tee.

He deemed it to be picturesque, although some of the immature fairways he described as rough. Faced by the challenge of planning a course among the sandhills, Braid used a mix of the two available design strategies. Fairways of some of the holes threaded their way along the valleys; whilst on others he utilised ridges that lay across the line of play. On these holes he was perpetuating blind shots, both off the tee and approaching the green. It also enabled him to include some of his favourite dog-leg holes. Many commentators have since described the characteristic S&A drive as being made through a narrow saddle in a ridge of sandhills. The size of these sandhills can be judged by the fact that from the hill alongside the 3rd tee it is possible to see the mountains of North Wales to the south and the Lake District to the north. At the Birkdale end of the course there was a triangle of holes, the 11th, 12th, and 13th, on relatively flat dune heath, which was known as 'Tattenham Corner' (Fig.27). This new course layout was to serve through the Ryder Cup years and survived substantially unaltered until the post-war period and many of the names given to holes at S&A date from the building of the new course.

26. A 1905 view across Birkdale Cemetery showing some of the dune land absorbed into Braid's new course.

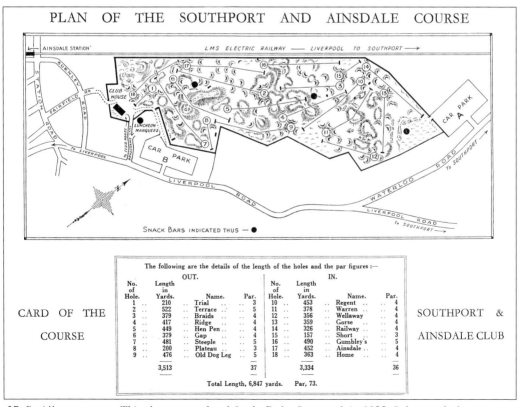

PLAN OF THE SOUTHPORT AND AINSDALE COURSE

The following are the details of the length of the holes and the par figures:—

CARD OF THE COURSE

SOUTHPORT & AINSDALE CLUB

No. of Hole.	Length in Yards.	Name.	Par.	No. of Hole.	Length in Yards.	Name.	Par.
		OUT.				IN.	
1	210	Trial	3	10	453	Regent	4
2	522	Terrace	5	11	378	Warren	4
3	379	Braids	4	12	356	Wellaway	4
4	417	Ridge	4	13	359	Gorse	4
5	449	Hen Pen	4	14	326	Railway	4
6	379	Gap	4	15	157	Short	3
7	481	Steeple	5	16	490	Gumbley's	5
8	200	Plateau	3	17	452	Ainsdale	4
9	476	Old Dog Leg	5	18	363	Home	4
	3,513		37		3,334		36

Total Length, 6,847 yards.   Par, 73.

27. Braid's new course. This plan was produced for the Ryder Cup match in 1933. Subsequently the course was so little changed that it was reproduced in the programmes of several post-war professional tournaments.

James Braid favoured naming the holes on courses he designed. The 3rd took his name, in the same way that the 16th retained the name of Gumbley, its creator. Other names, such as Terrace, Plateau, Ridge, Old Dog-Leg, Gorse, Warren, Railway, Steeple and Hen-Pen, reflect characteristics of the hole or adjoining features; whilst Regent was derived from the title of the Southport Regent Hockey and Tennis Club, to which S&A leased land alongside the railway, south of the new Hillside Station.

The site for the new clubhouse was at the extreme south end of the course. It was claimed that it was only 'A few minutes walk from Ainsdale Station.' Access from Liverpool Road was to be from a rough track – Bradshaw's Lane. This ancient fishermen's path continued across the links up to the railway, where a gated crossing gave access to 'The Hawes', an old dwelling now obscured from the course by tall trees. (See rear endpaper) The Club attempted unsuccessfully to secure a footbridge linking the course to Sandringham Road. This would have been convenient for members living west of the line, and for those who travelled to the course via Ainsdale Station. There was, however, a small branch railway line curving inland from the station sidings to serve Ainsdale Mill, and the Club had a private level crossing from Burnley Road. The clubhouse was to sit on an elevated plot to the south of Bradshaw's Lane, whilst immediately to the north of the lane was Booth's Farm, a rundown neglected thatched building surrounded by dilapidated wooden outbuildings, the whole sitting in about half an acre. From the beginning of negotiations, the Club had wished to include this insalubrious neighbour within its lease, but it was to be problems relating to this property that were to be the most contentious aspect of the whole affair.

Before leaving the era of the Liverpool Road clubhouse there remains an interesting royal question to be addressed. Did the Prince of Wales visit the clubhouse and take tea on its open balcony? Residents of the former clubhouse firmly believe this story that has been passed down by previous residents. The club archives do not contain any record of it, but the Prince did visit Southport in July 1921 as part of a four-day stay in Lancashire. There was much local criticism about the secrecy surrounding his itinerary, which, to the annoyance of civic dignitaries, was only received very shortly before the visit. The Prince's day started with a parade in the town centre, he then moved on to a reception at the Birkdale Town Hall. His route to Bootle took him down Liverpool Road, past the clubhouse and he was scheduled to make a brief stop at the corner of Liverpool Road and Mill Lane, where Ainsdale school children would be assembled. He was late arriving at this venue and his car did not stop. Newspaper accounts do not mention a visit to the clubhouse and a departure from the formal itinerary, but the opportunity was there and perhaps the evidence of oral history should be listened to in this instance.

Chapter Three
THE RYDER CUP YEARS

I am the oldest original member of the only golf club in the world that has housed the Ryder Cup twice. Some honour!

Walter Child 1946

Remarkably, although the work had only started in January 1923, the newly laid-out course was judged to be ready for play by September. To celebrate the opening a bogey competition for members was arranged. This was followed by an exhibition match, which involved E. Blackburn the Captain, who was a Lancashire county player, Sam Robinson, Percy Roberts the professional, and Richard Wright, the professional at the Southport Municipal course.

The 'bungalow style' of the single storey clubhouse made it unique amongst the golf clubs along the 'line', but fitted well into the locality. A Bolton firm completed the building in some twenty weeks at a cost of £4,887, which was £638 under the estimate (Fig.28). A mixed dinner was held in January 1925 to officially celebrate the opening. It also marked the resignation of Tom Forster, who had served as chairman of the Board since May 1908 (Fig.29). Just over one hundred guests sat down to eat in the main lounge and generous tributes were paid to Forster. Strangely, it seems that although he had been one of the original members, Tom had not been an active golfer.

28. The new clubhouse c.1925.

SOUTHPORT and AINSDALE
GOLF CLUB.

Opening Dinner

New Club House,
AINSDALE.

Presentation to the Chairman,
MR. T. W. FORSTER.

SATURDAY, 3rd JANUARY,
at 6 p.m. 1925,

Captain—MR. E. C. TAYLOR.

Wainwright & Son, Printers, 11, King St.

29. The Opening Dinner for the new clubhouse 1925.

Sharing the Club's administration with him had been John Linacre the secretary, who had also been in office since 1908. Sadly, the Booth's Farm issue had caused him to resign in 1924. This affair had rumbled on with the property being eventually excluded from the lease, as the tenant was protected under the Rent Restriction Act. It seems that there had been criticism of Linacre concerning his part in the negotiations. As a result he offered his resignation, which was accepted with regret. The landowner's agent later admitted that it was he, not Linacre, who was responsible for the problems that had arisen. In the event, Booth's Farm remained an obtrusive eyesore and the Club had to be content with getting it fenced off '…and so abate the nuisance caused by the tenant's goats.' Linacre had earlier presented an old 'cleek' to the Club for use as a trophy. (A 'cleek' was a shallow faced iron club with the approximate loft of a modern three iron) and he was elected an honorary life member in recognition of his services to the Club. Raising the £7,000, to pay for the changes at S&A, proved to be difficult. The Club received the sum of £1,770 from the Ministry of Transport for 'disturbance and compensation', and a further £1,600 from the sale of the former clubhouse. (It became a pair of semi-detached houses at 348 and 350 Liverpool Road.) It was expected that the balance of the money required would come from a bond issue. There were 800 bonds costing five-pounds each. The bonds would earn an annual interest of five per cent and would be repayable in ten years. Despite an intensive campaign of verbal and written exhortation less than £2,000 was raised, and in January 1925 the Club had to approach the bank and take out three £500 debentures to cover the remaining debts.

With the overdraft standing at £2,000 the Board promised to exercise prudence in its spending. One novel scheme to raise money was a joint venture with the railway company. Excursion tickets from Liverpool were available and the price included a green fee, lunch and tea.

Professional Percy Roberts's wooden shop had been transferred to the site of the new clubhouse, but in 1925 it was destroyed by fire and replaced by a new building. (See Fig.68) Percy later recalled how local youngsters had rummaged amongst the ashes and salvaged metal club heads. Apparently they fitted shafts and played with them. The members' cycle shed had also been moved. This proved to be inadequate to meet the demand and further accommodation was provided, behind the professional's new shop. The era of the motor-car was arriving and the demand for accommodation for cycles was diminishing. In the mid 1930s the cycle rack behind the professional's shop was replaced with a bench for the waiting caddies, and part of the cycle shed was adapted to serve as a shelter and toilet for them. The Club later approached the tenant of Booth's Farm for the use of part of his land for a car park.

Following the demise of full-time boy caddies, each club developed a cadre of adult caddies, who were classified and paid according to proficiency. In 1925 the S&A Board agreed a tariff of one shilling and seven pence (c. 8p) for a first-class caddie, and one shilling and one penny (less than 6p) for one of the second-class. In all cases the Club received one penny of the fee. Some schoolboys continued to caddie on a part-time basis.

With changes to the course came mechanisation. A hired horse had already replaced the aged pony, which had pulled the mowers for many years. Following the opening of the new course, it was decided that it too would be replaced, and two motor mowers were purchased. The Board reported a substantial increase in green fees from visitors, due, it was claimed, to '…the distinctive layout and excellent condition of the links, which have gained greatly in popularity.'

The first major competition to be held on the reconstructed course was an open thirty-six-hole medal played in 1925; Sam Robinson won the scratch prize. About every four years the Lancashire Union played one of its home matches at S&A, whilst the County Championship meeting was again held at S&A in 1928 when the champion was Sam Robinson. His arrival at S&A appears to have triggered an improvement in the standard of golf. In 1921 the Club came second in the Lancashire County Club Team Championship. It was won by S&A, for the first time, in 1928, and the team was again the runner-up in 1932. By the outbreak of World War Two, seven S&A members had followed Sam Robinson into the county team. (See p.173)

There were few professional tournaments in the 1920s, sponsorship was rare, and the economic climate was bleak. Leading professionals were content to receive the modest rewards to be derived from exhibition matches. Several such matches were staged at S&A. Walter Hagen was paid fifty pounds for playing in an exhibition match at S&A in 1926. It also involved two amateurs, Sam Robinson and Birkdale's Walker Cup player R.H. Hardman (Fig.30). Although the nett proceeds were intended for a local charity, the Club sustained a loss of over ten pounds in staging this match. In 1930 Sam Robinson and Percy Roberts faced the challenge of the Walker brothers – Cyril and Willie. Cyril, who weighed a mere 118 pounds, had learned his golf on the Lancashire coast before emigrating to America. The pinnacle of his professional career came when he won the United States Open Championship at the Oakland Hills Country Club in 1924 (Fig.31). Played in windy conditions, the field had included such eminent golfers as Bobby Jones and Walter Hagen.

The Club continued to support the fixtures of the Liverpool Alliance of Golfers and more prestigious national events were also attracted. In 1925 the course was used for three days for the northern qualifying rounds of the *News of the World* Golf Cup. This was the PGA match play championship, and the Club contributed fifty pounds towards the prize fund. An invitation was also issued for the *Daily Dispatch* to play its Northern Championship at S&A.

30. An exhibition match featuring Walter Hagen 1926

31. An exhibition match 1930.

The 1930s saw the emergence of S&A as a major venue for professional golf. Much of the credit for this development belongs to the Southport Council, and particularly to T.E. Wolstenholme, the authority's publicity manager. The Corporation recognised the growing popularity of golf as a sport, both for participants and for spectators. Professional tournaments were identified as a means of promoting golf as one of the town's attractions. The Publicity and Attractions Committee set up a Tournament Golf Committee, which included representatives of the four major local golf clubs. Along with the *Sunday Dispatch*, the Corporation sponsored the £1,500 Southport Professional Golf Tournament in 1930. In the following year this event was replaced by the Dunlop-Southport 1,500 Guineas Tournament. Dunlop and the Corporation shared the costs, estimated at £2,000 in 1931. The prize money was claimed to be the largest total offered for a tournament of this kind in Europe. It was sufficient to attract a field of 300, which included all the top British professionals and a small number from the United States, the Argentine and some European countries.

32. The Dunlop-Southport Tournament – Season Ticket 1931.

All four of Southport's leading clubs were, at different times, to be venues for the qualifying and final rounds of the Dunlop-Southport Tournament, although S&A was consistently one of the major participants (Fig.32). In preparation for the inaugural event, the course had been lengthened to 6,871 yards, an increase of some 400 yards. This was largely achieved by building some new tees, Sam Robinson advising on these alterations. Henry Cotton, who set a new course record of 68, won the tournament. As winner he collected a cheque for £300. Cotton also won this event at Hesketh in the following year. Bill Davies of Wallasey won in 1933, when the final rounds were again played at S&A. Henry Cotton was the runner-up, as he was in 1935. S&A was again the venue for the finals in

33. *The Dunlop-Southport Tournament 1936. Henry Cotton putting on the 6th green.*
Across the railway line Hawes House can be seen in the trees, and to the left former holes of the Hillside course.

1934, the winner being Alf Padgham, a success that he repeated when the finals returned to S&A in 1936. In this year Cotton set yet another course record with a round of 66 (Fig.33). Poppy Wingate, who worked as an assistant to her brother and was the first English lady playing professional, competed unsuccessfully in the qualifying rounds in 1937 and 1938, although she was not the back marker.

Cotton dominated British professional golf in this era, and was able to break the stranglehold that the Americans were exerting on the Open Championship, winning it on three occasions. He took British professional golf to a new level, both on and off the course. Through his game, style of living, manner and attitude, he helped to elevate the previously socially depressed status of professional golfers in this country. There had been only about eight domestic tournaments a year, and it was quite impossible for professionals to make a decent living from competitions alone. They had to rely on their regular income as club professionals. (A story that illustrates their contemporary standing involved Sam King, who played in the 1937 Ryder Cup. When playing in the Dunlop-Southport competition at S&A, he had lost a golf shoe. Only having one pair with him, he played wearing one golf shoe and one ordinary shoe.) Cotton's stubborn independent streak was well illustrated by his refusal to enter the 1938 Dunlop-Southport Tournament, the finals of which were again played at S&A. He described the event as a 'marathon', he particularly objected to the requirement to play in two qualifying rounds, prior to the seventy two-hole competition, with the possibility of a play-off over thirty-six holes. Henry Cotton was nominated for a knighthood, when such awards for professional sportsmen were rare. Sadly he died several days before the announcement was made in the 1988 New Year's Honours List.

Significant as the Club's contribution was in staging the Dunlop-Southport Tournaments, it rather pales when set alongside its Ryder Cup record. Sam Ryder was a successful businessman, who had been generously sponsoring professional golf throughout the 1920s. He also employed Abe Mitchell as his personal professional. Since 1924 American golfers had exercised a monopoly on the Open Championship, and Ryder hoped that his appointment of Mitchell, a leading British contender to break this grip, would give the player the time and opportunity to prepare an effective challenge for the title. Sam Ryder also presented a gold cup, costing a hundred guineas and topped by the model of a golfer, who looked suspiciously like Abe Mitchell, to be played for between a team of British and Irish professionals and one from the United States. Ryder attributed the original idea for the match to the Mere Golf Club professional George Duncan. Although there had been such an international match at Wentworth in 1926, it was considered not to be an official Ryder Cup match, as the American team was a scratch affair and had not been selected by the American PGA. The first official Ryder Cup match was staged at the Worcester Country Club in Massachusetts in 1927. Two years later the inaugural match in this country was played at the Moortown Golf Club. S&A was one of the clubs that made a donation of five guineas towards the expenses for the Ryder Cup match in the United States in 1931.

In November 1932, the secretary of the Professional Golfers' Association wrote to the Southport Town Council announcing that its committee had decided to play the 1933 Ryder Cup at Southport on a course and on dates to be arranged later. It now seems impossible that the arrangements could be so vague only a few months before the match was due to be played. Later, in a letter of thanks to the local authority, the PGA secretary identified T.E. Wolstenholme, the Publicity Manager, as the man responsible for bringing the event to Southport, it was he who had persuaded the Council to invite the PGA to stage the match here. Wolstenholme had already worked closely with S&A on other tournaments, and the finances for the Ryder Cup were to be managed by A.B. Dawson, who was both the Borough Treasurer and a future captain of S&A. The PGA's offer to play the game at S&A was received by the Board of Directors on 15th February, and it immediately accepted the invitation. The match was to be played in late June, following the Dunlop-Southport 1,500 Guineas Tournament in May. So it was that S&A became host for the second Ryder Cup match to be played in this country.

The Club immediately put in place a Ryder Cup Committee. Southport Corporation gave the Club £400 towards the cost of mounting the event. Little time was available to prepare the course but the Institute of Green Keeping Research at Bingley was consulted. Its report emphasized that S&A was a 'links' course and warned against the dangers of over-fertilising or watering the greens, thus inducing soft lush growth. The greenkeeper also had to deal with an excessive infestation of leather-jackets. To help with the preparation of the course a new motor tractor with a tipping body was purchased (Fig.34). New 'hole tins' and flags were also obtained.

Hosting this prestigious match taxed the facilities in the clubhouse. Limited dining accommodation was available, but marquees, to meet the demand for catering, were erected in the area where members now park cars. The clubhouse did not include a bar at this time and the steward

34. Railwaymen and greenkeepers look on whilst the Reliance Garage (Liverpool Road roundabout)
staff unload the new Pattisson motor tractor in front of the 7th tee.
Percy Roberts, wearing plus fours, casts a professional eye over the operation.

brought drinks on a tray from the still-room to the lounge. This was an arrangement that worked in a gentlemen's club, but was hardly appropriate for a major international sporting event.

American professionals were already leaving their British and Irish counter parts behind in terms of earnings, status and golfing achievement. One journalist commented on the smart outfits of the visiting team and described the home team as looking '...a motley crew'. The PGA had nominated J.H. Taylor, one of golf's 'Great Triumvirate', as the first non-playing captain. He was one of the founders of the PGA. The legendary Walter Hagen led the United States team (Fig.35). The captain of the British 1931 Ryder Cup team had described Hagen as: 'Sir Walter, the prince of professional golfers.' The pre-match relationship between the 1933 captains was so bad, however, that Taylor threatened to abandon the match before a ball had been struck. It seems that the American captain was playing mind games by keeping him waiting. Taylor had been making desperate attempts to contact him in order to settle the match pairings.

The match was played over just two days. The outstanding British player Henry Cotton, the professional at the Royal Waterloo Club in Belgium, was not selected because the PGA rules restricted participation to professionals

35. *The two Ryder Cup captains with Samuel Ryder. J.H. Taylor (left) finally greets Walter Hagen.*

working in Britain. On the first day (Monday) there were four foursome games and on the second day (Tuesday) eight singles games. All the games were contested over thirty-six holes. The match was played in glorious sunshine. Percy Roberts, the professional, was the starter and Sam Robinson was in charge of crowd control on the 1st tee, where his stentorian cry of 'Stand please' was more a command than a request. There was no practice ground at this time and players' pre-play preparation was restricted to swinging a club and practising short pitch shots on the small area of ground to the right of the 1st tee. Observers said that the animosity between Hagen and Taylor was apparent in the manner in which Hagen made practice swings perilously close to Taylor. A single stall, which was provided by a local outfitter and devoted to the sale of golf clothing, shared this area along with a game stall, which would have looked at home at a church fete. (At the back of a netting stall was a screen with six pockets, punters had to pitch five of six golf balls into the pockets in order to win a five pounds prize.) The average age of the British team was thirty-four and Taylor was concerned about their fitness. He ordered a compulsory early morning run and fitness training on the beach, under the direction of a physical training instructor from St Andrews University. Although sixty-two-years of age, Taylor, a noted disciplinarian, led by example, taking part in the run.

Over 2,000 spectators set off to follow the first match, the pairing of Percy Alliss (Peter's father) and Charlie Whitcombe playing Gene Sarazen and Walter Hagen. The second match, which involved Abe Mitchell, also attracted a large crowd (Fig.36). Mitchell, who was approaching fifty, was a reluctant member of the team. He was one of the few professionals who continued to use hickory-shafted clubs after the introduction of metal shafts in the late 1920s. Nevertheless he was to win both of his games, including a sensational recovery to win by 9 and 8 in his singles match. It was members acting as marshals who ushered the numerous spectators around the course, or as Henry Longhurst, a former Cambridge University golf captain, for whom this match was his first press assignment, wrote, '...they were herded, cajoled and threatened about the course.' To help the stewards to form barriers they carried long bamboo poles with small red and white pennants attached. It was the appearance of these poles, and the fact that the stewards were mobile, following the matches around the course, that led to them being dubbed the 'Southport Lancers' (Fig.37). The pennants of the lancers are evident on almost all the photographs of the match. The crowds on day two were even larger than those present on the first day. The overall official attendance was put at 14,242, but it was believed that many others gained entry. It was not only the golf that led to the arrival of such numbers.

36. Abe Mitchell putting on Braid's 2nd green.

37. 'Southport Lancers' assembled in front of the professional's shop and ready to move off.

38. The Prince of Wales, accompanied by Paul Carter the S&A Captain, seeking the sanctuary of the clubhouse.

39. The master scoreboard as the match reached its climax and the result was still in doubt.

The match was watched by HRH the Prince of Wales, the future Edward VIII who was the President of the Professional Golfers' Association. The Prince had been expected to fly into Liverpool airport and to arrive at the course at approximately two o'clock. In the event he travelled to Merseyside by car in order to take lunch in the French Restaurant of Liverpool's then prestigious Adelphi Hotel, and only arrived at S&A at about three-thirty. He was there in time to watch the last pair on the 1st hole. Such was the huge crowd following the Prince, that normal play was impossible. He attempted to watch some play around the 6th, 7th, 8th, and 16th holes, but his presence caused serious hold ups and he returned to the sanctuary of the clubhouse (Fig.38).

After two days in which fortunes of the teams had ebbed to and fro, the outcome of the match came down to the result of the last singles game (Fig.39). Syd Easterbrook, a little-known twenty-seven-year-old English club professional, who had originally been nominated as a reserve for the match, and the American Densmore Shute, a frequent and recent tournament winner, came to the final hole with their game all square. As this was the only game left on the course, the spectators were all clambering to gain vantage points around the 18th. Both of the competitors drove into bunkers and played the hole scrappily to reach the green in three. It appears that Shute probably didn't fully appreciate the overall position of the match and that a half would be sufficient for the United States, the holders, to retain the trophy. His captain was not at the greenside, he was watching from the clubhouse in the company of the Prince. A fierce competitor, Hagen apparently thought of leaving the clubhouse to make certain that Shute understood the position, but courtesy prevailed and he remained inside. In the event Shute putted boldly for a win and finished five or six feet past the hole (Fig.40). He missed the return leaving Easterbrook with what Longhurst described as '…a four foot putt with a nasty left-hand borrow…He holed it like a man.' The home team had won the hole with a five against a six and thus took the Ryder Cup for the second time (Figs. 41 & 42).

This narrow defeat came as an unexpected shock to the Americans, who had won the 1931 match so easily. In an article in the *New York Sun*, its golf correspondent was critical of the quality of the home professionals, and also of the size of the greens at S&A. He wrote that:

> The relatively inaccurate British shot makers can stray twenty yards off line and
> still finish somewhere on these polo-field greens, whereas in this country (ie
> U.S.A.) the invaders would be up to their necks in the bottle neck pits (ie
> bunkers) which eat into the flanks of the greens.

40. *The last rites – the final match on the green at the 36th hole. Shute about to putt, Easterbook watches and waits.*

*41. A section of the crowd in front of the clubhouse for the presentation of the Cup.
In the background is the 1933 version of the 'tented village'.*

42. The presentation and 'Three cheers for the Prince.'

American pride was somewhat restored when two members of their team went on to tie for the lead in the Open Championship, which was played the following week at St Andrews. The play-off was won by Densmore Shute, to give him some consolation after his dreadful experience on the last hole at S&A. Peter Alliss later wrote that despite enjoying an outstanding career, Shute is principally remembered as the man who lost the Ryder Cup, a reputation that he himself was to share. Financially the Ryder Cup match had been a success and there was a substantial surplus to fund sending a British team to America in 1935, when the home team regained the trophy.

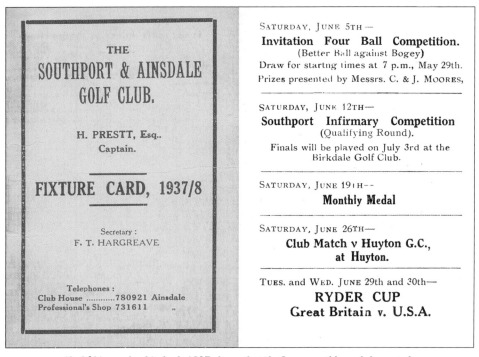

THE

SOUTHPORT & AINSDALE GOLF CLUB.

H. PRESTT, Esq..
Captain.

FIXTURE CARD, 1937/8

Secretary :
F. T. HARGREAVE

Telephones :
Club House ....780921 Ainsdale
Professional's Shop 731611   ,,

SATURDAY, JUNE 5TH —
Invitation Four Ball Competition.
(Better Ball against Bogey)
Draw for starting times at 7 p.m., May 29th.
Prizes presented by Messrs. C. & J. MOORES,

SATURDAY, JUNE 12TH—
Southport Infirmary Competition.
(Qualifying Round).
Finals will be played on July 3rd at the Birkdale Golf Club.

SATURDAY, JUNE 19TH—
Monthly Medal

SATURDAY, JUNE 26TH—
Club Match v Huyton G.C., at Huyton.

TUES. and WED. JUNE 29th and 30th—
**RYDER CUP
Great Britain v. U.S.A.**

43. S&A membership book 1937 shows that the June monthly medal was to be played on the course just over a week prior to the Ryder Cup match.

Driven by Southport Council's determination to be involved in promoting top professional golf the Ryder Cup Match returned to S&A in 1937. This meant that the Club hosted two of the first three matches to be contested in this country. On this occasion the Club had slightly longer notice than in 1933, it was all of eight months. The members' fixture card shows how little disturbance the inclusion of the Ryder Cup Match made to the normal programme (Fig.43). Still a two-day competition, it was played on a Tuesday and Wednesday, with the American team arriving in Southport on the previous Thursday. Ever the extrovert, Walter Hagen, the American non-playing captain announced: 'We are bringing a winning team. In fact, we only brought the cup over for you to get a look at it and see for yourselves we are taking good care of it.' This was the Ryder Cup version of his usual pre-tournament taunt to fellow competitors of 'Waal, who's gonna be second?'

The Club again had a sub-committee with responsibility for planning the event. Mr. F.T. Hargreaves, the honorary secretary, was irritated at criticism levelled at the Club on account of the steep increase in entry charges since 1933, as such decisions were completely in the hands of the Professional Golfers' Association. There was also criticism of the stewarding of the 1933 match, when it was charged that both players and spectators had been aggravated by the marshals' actions. Hargreaves responded that there would be only about 300 rather than 500 stewards, and they would be deployed at fixed points rather than being allowed to run all over the course and thus obstruct some spectators' view. Without the pressure that had resulted from the visit of the Prince of Wales in 1933, the 'Southport Lancers' had been stood down, or at least reined in. Poor weather also affected the attendance, which dropped to 8,918.

On this occasion the home team included Henry Cotton, who had moved to a British club. In practice he had done a 64 and Longhurst later wrote that there was '...an air of restrained optimism, in which I shared at that time.' Mindful of their defeat in 1933, the Americans had brought what they considered to be a very strong team. On the first day the sun shone, the ground was baked hard and a wind of almost gale force was blowing. Recalling the lack of opportunity for pre-match practice in 1933, Hagen took his side out on the course early on the opening day. In the foursome matches that followed, the United States established a lead of two and a half to one and a half. On the morning of the second day the players were greeted by heavy driving rain, conditions, it might be argued, that should have favoured the home players. In the event the Americans were more effective in keeping the ball under control and putted better to retain the cup with a score of eight games to two, with two games halved. It was their first Ryder Cup victory on British soil. The match saw the emergence of one home hero, Dai Rees, a '...highly combative little Welshman' who was making his Ryder Cup debut. Although one of two assistant professionals in the team, he was responsible for one and a half of the British team's meagre points total (Fig.44). In his speech at the presentation of the trophy, Charles Whitcombe, the home team captain, acknowledged that it was a team event, but picked out the performance of twenty-four-year-old Rees, the youngest member of his team, for special praise. In his remarks, J.H. Taylor, the chairman of the PGA, expressed the hope that they would be invited back to

44. Welsh supporters chair Dai Rees back to the clubhouse after his victory over Byron Nelson.

S&A in four years time, when the Ryder Cup Match returned to these islands. The Chairman of the Southport Publicity and Attractions Committee later suggested that as Southport had done more than any other local authority in Great Britain to support professional golf, it was '…in an extremely strong position to make representations to the PGA to choose Southport for the next Ryder Cup Match.' It is possible that without the intervention of World War Two, S&A might have emerged as a regular venue for this event.

In a letter written to the S&A captain, Christopher Walker, in 2002, the American Byron Nelson, who had played in the 1937 match as a twenty-five-year-old, revealed a few of his memories. Apart from the poor weather, he recalled that to their surprise, the wives of the American players were not allowed into the clubhouse and were huddled outside in the cold and the wet. It seems that it was only due to the good offices of the Mayoress of Southport that they eventually gained sanctuary inside. British golf had not yet come to terms with the involvement of ladies in golf. Indeed Longhurst, a young bachelor, commenting on the presence of the American wives, argued that it would be an encumbrance equivalent roughly to conceding two shots a round. Much later, in a more politically correct age, he conceded that this forecast was '…as inaccurate as it was ungallant.'

For most professionals, playing in minor regional competitions was the height of their aspiration. As early as 1931 S&A staged such a competition for the Liverpool Golfers' Alliance. An S&A member put up what was described as 'a substantial sum' (£25), for competition amongst the Merseyside professionals. In 1933 the Alliance played a foursome bogey competition, involving amateurs, at S&A. This was won by a home pair of Max Hargreave (1) and Harry Kipling, the senior assistant professional who later died as a prisoner of war on the infamous Burma-Siam railway.

The Club was regularly involved in hosting Lancashire Ladies' County Golf Association events. The Association successfully asked for the use of the course for their championship in 1925, and county matches were played in 1926, 1928 and again in 1931. It was probably economics that dictated that in 1931 the Lancashire and the Cumberland and Westmoreland teams should play two matches on the same day, counting one as the home encounter and the other the away return fixture.

In 1936, the premier national ladies' event came to S&A in the form of the British Ladies' Amateur Open Golf Championship (Fig.45). The occasion

45. British Ladies' Championship 1936, the competitors outside the clubhouse. S&A's Welsh international Marjorie Barron can be seen standing at the extreme right of the group.

was made memorable by the participation of the American Curtis Cup team including Glenna Collett Vare, who dominated ladies' golf in America for many years. She won the United States Women's Amateur Championship on six occasions and captained the American Curtis Cup team five times.

The presence of this golfing great was somewhat overshadowed by the appearance of probably the most extraordinary character ever to have played ladies' championship golf. She was Gloria Minoprio, the daughter of a Liverpool merchant of Italian extraction. What made her a curiosity was the fact that she attempted to prove that championship golf could be successfully played using only one club. Her chosen club was a cleek, a rather straight-faced iron, which she described as being '...entirely unadapted'. Although only using this one club her caddie carried a duplicate as insurance against breakage along with a bag of balls.

Her appearance added to the air of mystery. She was tall, slim and dark and wore dark clothing from head to foot – a torque, close fitting tunic and

46. Gloria Minoprio.

immaculately cut guardsman-type trousers and white gloves. Her Championship debut at Westward Ho!, three years earlier, was the first occasion that any lady competitor in a major championship had played in trousers but there was nothing in the rules to stop her, although the LGU did issue a proclamation deploring '...any departure from the traditional costume of the game.' Her face was '...ghostly pale from white make-up, save for the scarlet gash of her mouth.' (Fig.46) Eleanor Helm of *The Morning Post* likened her to a stage Mephistopheles.

Miss Minoprio was in fact an accomplished magician and played golf as if in a trance, staring straight ahead and never speaking, other than to say 'Thank you' at the end of the game. She claimed that her chosen club was '...tamed and docile' in her hands. Her unconventional manner of addressing the ball, by waving the club to and fro over it, compounded the overall air of mystery. Nevertheless, she could play golf. It appears that she had a golf handicap of four having received regular lessons from the professional at Huntercombe in Oxfordshire, where her husband rented a cottage alongside the course. To practise escaping from bunkers with her cleek, he had one built in their garden. Between 1931 and 1939 she was a little known member of the Littlestone-on-Sea Golf Club. In the 1934 championship she won her first match against a very nervous opponent before succumbing in the next round to the eventual champion. The *Sunday Graphic* reporting on the 1936 qualifying rounds at S&A judged that 'the greatest performance of the whole day was the 84 of the 'one club' Miss Minoprio.' The *Daily Mail* correspondent described her as 'a graceful player...who wielded her single iron club brilliantly.' Henry Longhurst wrote of her that: 'Never in the history of women's golf has a competitor caused such a sensation.' If her purpose was to secure attention and publicity she succeeded, but she did not appear to attempt to cash in on her celebrity. To understand the Minoprio phenomenon, one perhaps needs to know more about the role played by her wealthy, but elderly husband. She continued to have her annual tilt at the British and English titles until 1939.

There was further drama during the semi-finals of the 1936 Championship at S&A when a stretch of long grass and gorse bushes, alongside the 7th hole, caught fire (Fig.47). Fortunately the resulting cloud of dense smoke did not disrupt the competition as the two matches had already passed this point. Pam Barton, a highly talented nineteen-year-old English international, who had been the runner-up in the previous two years, eventually won the championship. Two members of S&A, Miss Shaw and Mrs. Douglas, played on the two qualifying days, but did not progress to the match play rounds.

On the domestic front, the lady members of S&A were enjoying a busy golfing calendar, including matches against the Formby Ladies, Hillside and Preston clubs. In 1926 a ladies' invitation fourball competition was introduced. In the same year the Board agreed to purchase the periodical *Eve and Bystander* for the ladies' lounge. Three years later S&A hosted this magazine's popular annual 'Eve Ladies' Northern Foursomes'. Although it was a handicap event it attracted some of the country's outstanding golfers. The winners were the English internationals Doris Fowler and Phyllis

47. Attempting to beat out a fire during the Dunlop-Southport Tournament 1955.
Dune heath with heather is vulnerable to fire during very dry spells.

Lobbett of the North Hants Club (Fig. 48). A number of S&A members played, including at least five past lady captains. Three of these home club pairings made it through to the second round, including Marjorie Wren, the current lady captain, and her partner (Fig.49). Although this was the end of the road for these modestly handicapped players, they all received the customary and much prized *Eve* gift of a box of bon-bon chocolates when they were defeated.

Miss Wren was a frequent winner of scratch and later handicap trophies. She won the Hall Cup in 1920 and the Lady Captain's Prize in 1935. Off the course she was a stalwart committee worker over many years. In 1938 Trud Arthur, who had partnered her in the *Eve* tournament, won the Lancashire County Ladies' Golf Association's Silver Division Golfing Challenge.

During the 1930s, a golfing star, who was to become S&A's most distinguished lady player, emerged. It was in 1928 that young Marjorie Barron won the Championship of Glamorgan. The following year she played in the British Ladies' Championship and made her debut for Wales

48. Eve Ladies' Northern Foursomes 1929. One of the winning pair, English international Mrs. Lobbett, putting on Gumbley's. Braid had lengthened this hole by using what had been the 9th green. (Compare with Fig.15)

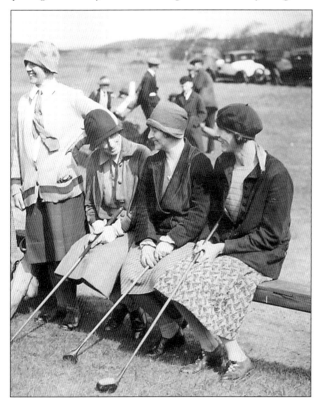

49. Eve Ladies' Northern Foursomes 1929. In the middle of the three ladies seated waiting on the 1st tee was S&A Lady Captain Marjorie Wren, to her left was her partner Trud Arthur.

50. Marjorie Barron (left) leaving the 18th green at St Andrews, when the British Ladies' Championship and the home internationals were played there in 1929. Andrew Kirkaldy, the R&A's first Club Professional, is at her side. The other player is the American star Glenna Collett Vare.

in the home internationals, which were run in conjunction with it (Fig.50). She held her place in the team for eight of the following ten years, and played in all three games when the home internationals were played at S&A in 1936, winning against Ireland and losing to English and Scottish opponents. (See Fig.45) At this time she was an active member of the New Highwood Club in Sussex, but by 1938 she was a member of S&A, where she won the Hall Cup. In 1939 she won the Captain's Prize and was to become a major force in the Club.

The ladies' section was prospering, but the number was still restricted to 120 and as early as 1923 the Board decided that vacancies should be reserved for relatives of male members. In 1930, the waiting list for lady associate members was closed, excepting for family members, or candidates with a handicap of sixteen or less. It is perhaps significant that prior to 1930 a third of the lady captains were spinsters, but since that year there has only been one. The S&A ladies enjoyed the benefit of some interesting local rules that allowed them to shelter from rain during competitions, as long as they didn't return to the clubhouse, and in specified cases of '...fearsome bunkers and ditches' they were allowed to take relief without penalty.

The venue for the men's annual dinner, which had originally been held in the clubhouse, moved between the Royal and Victoria Hotels before settling at the Prince of Wales (Fig.51). H. Andrews donated a trophy for competition amongst the veterans in 1928. Whilst captain in 1933, Paul Carter presented a silver salver for a competition to raise funds for the local infirmary. Each of the local clubs held a qualifying round and the top four competitors from each club contested a final. The competition continued to be played up until 1948. 1938 saw the return of the Lancashire Union to play its championship at S&A. The only inter-club match listed in the 1939 S&A fixture card was a home and away match with the Huyton and Prescot Club. A *Tatler* cartoon appeared to reflect a settled nature of life at S&A in 1939, with no suggestion of the international storm clouds that were gathering (Fig.52).

As was evident in the career of Sam Robinson, experience as a caddie introduced golf to a wider social audience and created an appetite for playing the game. Following the return of the servicemen from the First World War, the Artisan Golf Association was formed in 1921. One of its principal sponsors was J.H. Taylor. Artisan golfers enjoyed restricted free, or very cheap, golf in return for performing duties on the course. From 1922, the S&A Board received a series of letters from this association, enquiring about the possibility of forming an artisan section, but no action was taken. However, in 1935 such

51. The Annual Dinner at the Prince of Wales Hotel 1935.

52. *A cartoon from* **The Tatler** *June 1939.*

a group was formed. Was it a coincidence that J.H. Taylor had recently captained the British team at the Ryder Cup match at S&A and was chairman of the PGA, which would determine the venue for the 1937 match? The section was initially restricted to sixteen members, who had to be '…bona fide workmen' living in Ainsdale or Birkdale. Their duties were principally to act as rangers on the course, in order to reduce trespass. Armlets and badges were bought for them; the armlets had to be worn when on duty and the badges when playing (Fig.53). The Board bought an asbestos hut to serve as their club room and a grant was given towards its fitting out and furnishing. In return, the duties were expanded to include work on the course, particularly weeding. The Club Captain in 1937, Harry Prestt, a wealthy town-centre grocer who travelled in a chauffeur-driven Rolls Royce, presented a silver cup to the artisans for an annual competition, and in the following year, they were allowed to arrange matches with other artisan clubs.

An interesting aspect of course management in this era was the policy of planting as many trees as became available. Green Committee minutes gratefully recorded planting gifts of what are now regarded as weed trees - poplars and sycamores. (See Fig.36) White 'driving posts' to mark 200 yards were

53. An S&A Artisan badge.

installed and the original Ryder Cup tees were marked by red pyramid blocks bearing the legend – 'Ryder Cup Tee'. Playing off these tees came to be a feature of golf at S&A, especially for visitors. Special 'Ryder Cup Score Cards' were produced for those who wished to meet this challenge.

Harry Mann, a retired solicitor now living in Tasmania, who was a junior member in the early 1930s, recalls that: 'There were, perhaps, half a dozen junior members.' These sons and daughters of members included the two children of the secretary. Harry remembers the strictly enforced restrictions placed on juniors, reporting that they '…were tolerated but not encouraged.' It seems that there might have been something of a sea change in the later 1930s. As Sam Robinson's illustrious career began to wane, so a new young star, Tom Hiley, appeared in the S&A firmament. The Hiley family had migrated to Southport from Keighley in the early 1930s. Living on the newly built Waterloo Road, their back garden overlooked the S&A course, whilst their business, Ainsdale Laundry, had a towering chimney that could be seen from almost every point on the course. The laundry was on Liverpool Road, between Burnley Road and Bradshaw's Lane. Millbourne Lodge, a block of flats, now occupies the site. After his father became a member of the club, Tom joined as a schoolboy in about 1934. The professional, Percy Roberts, took a close interest in the development of this promising young pupil who was naturally left-handed. Percy turned him round to play right-handed; this decision might have had more to do with economics and the availability of left-handed clubs than it did to some physiological theory. Percy had two young sons, who were also learning the game at this time. In 1935 Tom won the Junior Members' Challenge Cup with a nett score of 66, playing off a handicap of twenty-three. This trophy had been introduced in 1929 to encourage junior members. Incidentally, it was won by the professional's son Geoffrey in 1937, and in the following year by his brother Gerald. (Gerald was later to be an assistant to Percy, but died at a tragically early age in 1945.) These junior members, whose access to the course was restricted, also played along with other local boys on the three-hole 'sand course' that they had laid out on the waste land behind the clubhouse, the area now occupied by Berwick Avenue and Bradshaw's Lane.

Within a year of his first success in the club event of 1935, Tom Hiley was playing in the British Boys' Championship at Birkdale, a tournament won by the great Irish golfer, James 'The Loop' Bruen. Tom successfully negotiated three rounds, having 'swamped' one opponent '…by the excellence of his play', but it was his habit of always wearing his school cap when he played, that attracted the attention of newspaper reporters. Sixteen-year-old Tom was a pupil at Bickerton House, a long since departed private school in Birkdale. Jackie Wroe, another local boy who was to join S&A after the war, also played in this Championship, but lost in the first round.

After his success at Birkdale, and with his handicap down to five, Tom was allowed to transfer from junior to full membership, a move normally restricted to over twenty-one-year-olds. This gave him access to club competitions and also allowed him to play in the Liverpool Alliance (Fig.54). Appearing in these events gave him not only the experience of playing alongside professionals, but also regular practice at competing. His progress was rapid and he was selected to play for the English Boys' Team in 1937 and 1938. He entered the Lancashire Championship, which was played at Southport and Ainsdale in 1938 (Fig.55). In the qualifying round Sam Robinson led the field, again winning the Rayner Batty Trophy, but in the match play stage Tom reached the final to be narrowly defeated by an experienced opponent. He was also the leading amateur in a distinguished field in the Liverpool Golf Championship. In the following year with his handicap down to scratch he entered the Amateur Championship, conveniently played at Royal Liverpool. There he fought his way through five rounds before succumbing to the final winner, a Scottish international. His play in this tournament attracted much attention. Fred Pignon, the golf correspondent of the *Daily Mail* wrote:

> This was youth's proud day at the Amateur Golf Championship at the Royal Liverpool Club's sun-baked links. Two nineteen year old players, James Bruen of Cork and Tom Hiley of Southport (sic.), and Kenneth Thorn, the seventeen year old Essex Boys' Champion, stole most of the admiration of the big crowd for their amazing feats of golfing skill.

Tom's reward was to be selected as a reserve for the English team in the 1939 home international series. Sadly, the war clouds that had been gathering led to the cancellation of these matches and with the outbreak of war, in September, all competitive representative golf ceased. Earlier in the year Tom had won the Lancashire Union's Bell Trophy at Lytham with his partner Len 'Siege Gun' Birkett. He also won the Club's Scratch Prize in 1939, and

54. Liverpool Alliance at Hillside c.1938. Tom Hiley driving off the 17th (now 10th) tee. His regular Alliance partner, Jack Clough the licensee of the Bold Hotel, is stood hands on hips.

then the Captain's Prize in 1940 and 1941, before his war service abroad lost him several years at a critical stage in what was already a promising golf career.

Whilst rejoicing in the emergence of Tom Hiley as the Club's leading player, it is perhaps appropriate to close Part One of this history by noting that in 1939, Sam Robinson won the Veterans' Trophy with a score of 74, off a handicap of plus two.

55. Tom Hiley probably drawn in 1938, when he reached the final of the Lancashire Championship. Note the chimney of the family laundry.

PART TWO
1939-2006

Chapter Four

THE GUARDIANS AND THE COURSE

Now it seems – or at least when the lease runs out – everything is indeed to be spoiled at S&A. The course is to be acquired, appropriated, or taken over, or seized according to how you look at it…and what is politely called 'developed'.
Henry Longhurst **Sunday Times** 1959

With the country again involved in a war, life at Southport and Ainsdale took on a completely different aspect. Many members were absent, serving in the armed forces and the Board granted them continuing membership, without the payment of fees. The courtesy of the course was extended to visiting members of His Majesty's Forces, merchant seamen and to allied servicemen. The majority of the players who availed themselves of this concession were American airmen staying at Birkdale's requisitioned Palace Hotel, whilst having a break from flying operational missions over Europe. Other regular visitors were American soldiers from Huyton, naval personnel from HMS Queen Charlotte, the training unit for maritime gunners at the top of Shore Road, and airmen from Woodvale. In 1944 over 4,000 courtesy rounds were played on the course. Many of these visiting servicemen were golfing novices and the Green Committee wanted the Club to charge a modest green fee to cover the damage being caused to the course, a request that the Board rejected.

The Club's normal social calendar was much restricted and events such as the annual dinner were suspended (Fig.56). The limited supply of alcohol and cigarettes had to be rationed; the serving of double whiskies was discontinued and the Board decided that, in the interest of equality, part of the cigarette quota should be allocated to lady members. As a consequence of petrol rationing new racks for storing bicycles were purchased, and A.B. Dawson, the Captain in 1942, declared that he was '…the only captain who commenced his year coming to the Club in his motor car and finished the year using a bicycle.'

The shortage of petrol also hampered the staff in tending the course. As in World War One there was pressure to help in food production. A dairy farmer, in Liverpool Road, was allowed to pasture twenty cows on the course, for which he paid twenty pounds a year. As with most golf clubs, the loss in income from fees and in the clubhouse posed serious financial problems but these were eased by the Estate's agreement to temporarily reduce the rent.

After much of mainland Europe fell to the Panzer blitzkrieg, the German army stood on the Channel coast poised ready for invasion of these islands. As part of the preparation to repel possible airborne glider attack, obstacles to landing were erected on open flat spaces. At S&A, these took the form of double trenches dug by members across some fairways, including the 2nd and the 4th. (Golfers were allowed a free drop from these hazards.) In 1940 Royal

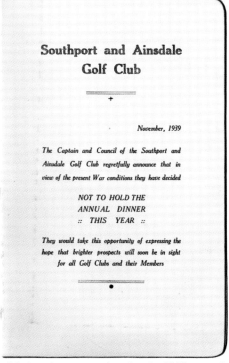

56. A notice announcing that the 1939 annual dinner was not to be held.

Engineers built a concrete base for a searchlight, which operated with anti-aircraft gun batteries as part of the local air defences. The flat area that marks this site can still be found to the west of the 9th fairway. The RAF built a road, north of the cemetery, to link with Liverpool Road. There was also a Fire Guard hut by the 13th tee. Southport did not suffer the sustained aerial bombardment experienced by Liverpool and Bootle. Bombing was restricted to odd incidents, mainly cases of aircraft returning after raiding Merseyside and jettisoning the remains of their bomb loads prior to following their escape flight path, north up the Ribble valley and across the Pennines to the North Sea. A few small bombs, including a stick of incendiaries, did fall on the course. There is a frequently repeated tale of an unexploded bomb still buried somewhere between the 3rd and 4th holes. By late 1944 the threat of air raids had diminished and the sandbags piled in front of the clubhouse were removed.

As early as 1943, the Town Council was anticipating the end of hostilities and addressing the issues of post war re-construction, particularly the provision of housing. In the summer of that year, there were rumours circulating that the Corporation was again interested in obtaining part of the course for public housing. To understand this chapter in the Club's history, it is necessary to recognise the status of the principal players in the drama. The Southport and Ainsdale Golf Club Limited leased the course. Landownership had earlier moved to the Ince-Blundell Estate, which, like all landowners, was reluctant to tie–up such a large area of land with a long lease, whilst it still entertained any prospect that it might later be able to use the land for more profitable residential development. If planning permission for building could be obtained, the value of the land would soar. The third player was the Southport Corporation, with which the Club had enjoyed such an excellent relationship whilst sharing the mounting of professional golf at S&A through the 1930s. The Corporation's role was critical as it was responsible for planning in the borough.

A dramatic headline in the *Southport Visiter* in January 1944 posed the question: 'Is the Golf Club (S&A) Doomed?' The article speculated that the course '…may fall within the scope of portended developments by Southport Corporation Town Planning and Improvement Committee.' It seems that the Estate was sceptical about the Corporation's intentions, possibly believing that zoning as building land would not free its land up for the landowner to undertake profitable private development, but for the Corporation to use for the necessary expansion in public housing provision after the end of hostilities. In April the Club received a letter from the Southport Corporation requesting a meeting. The stated purpose was to discuss the Club's lease. The Board met a deputation of two members of the Council and the Borough Engineer, Mr. Bunting. Mr. Bunting was the father of Tom a future captain and chairman of the Club. The spokesman for the Corporation was Alderman Aveling, the chairman of the Town Planning and Improvement Committee and a man who believed that golf clubs were important for Southport. He reminded members of the Board that thirty years ago the government had advised the Weld-Blundell Estate, as it then was, that the area of the S&A golf course was scheduled for eventual use as building land. He added that he personally thought that the Club would initially lose the 12th and 13th holes, at the end of the present lease in 1950. The 12th green and the 13th tee were the apex of a triangle of holes, which had the 11th hole as its base and formed 'Tattenham Corner'. (See Figs. 27 & 58) This land, adjacent to Ryder Crescent, would be used to continue the successful residential development that had already reached the margin of the course by 1938.

Aveling obviously wanted S&A to survive as a strong golf club, if possible with an enhanced championship course, and he posited two possible strategies for the Club. The first was to accept the loss of some land at the northern margin of the course and endeavour to negotiate an extension of the lease for the remainder, together with the acquisition of additional land to offset the loss. This would be a difficult prospect given the state of development around the course, also by following this route the threat of losing further land at a later date would still hang over the Club. His second suggestion was to obtain a lease for an area of the sand dunes north of Shore Road, between the two railway lines, which he believed could be secured for a mere 'peppercorn rent'. This was the land that Charles Weld-Blundell had tried unsuccessfully to lease to the Liverpool Banking and Insurance Golf Club in 1906.

This was not dune heath; it was the southern extension of the tall dune system in which (Royal) Birkdale had fashioned its majestic links. (See Fig.2) The Board was attracted by the possibility of having enough land of this quality on which to build a first-class championship course. There was press speculation about there being enough ground for two courses, with the possibility of establishing a ladies' course. The Club was further encouraged when it received a letter from the Town Clerk in December 1944, in which he indicated that the Town Planning and Improvement Committee was prepared to give favourable consideration to the use of this area of sandhills for the purpose of a golf course. In fact, despite some councillors' opposition to the granting of long leases to golf clubs, the Town Council approved, in principle, that in view of the capital costs that would be incurred, the Club should be allowed to have a two nines (99 years) lease on the land, much longer than the leases normally allowed to golf clubs in this area. In putting his case in the preceding debate, Aveling, who was later thanked by the S&A Board '...for the unsparing manner in which he had always looked after the Club's interests', described the Club as '...one of the town's finest assets.' The Club was asked to submit detailed proposals for the layout of the proposed course. Surprisingly, perhaps, the commission to prepare this scheme was given to J.A. Steer, the professional at Lytham Green Drive, who had a modest regional portfolio of planning golf construction work.

Steer's design was for a championship golf course of approximately 6,700 yards length on 164 acres. The site for a clubhouse was agreed, and Steer offered two alternative designs for the course. The first plan involved extensive earth moving to create fairways 'at will'. He estimated the cost of such a course as almost £62,000. His second alternative was to let the fairways follow '...the natural trend of the sandhills', as at Birkdale, which, he suggested, would be about £14,000 cheaper. It seems that the Club was so confident that this scheme would go through that the secretary told a

57. In addition to the distinguished international golfers, this 1952 cartoon includes a number of officials who were influential in shaping the destiny of S&A at a critical period of its history.

Daily Express golf columnist that '…the present course is scheduled for development as a residential area.' He even informed him that the clubhouse would make an excellent convalescent home and had a flat, which could be used by the matron. It was at this point, however, that the Estate pulled the rug from under the whole scheme. The solicitor for the Ince-Blundell Estate, made it abundantly clear that, although the Estate had no immediate prospect of developing this site for residential purposes, it was opposed to allowing the Club to lease so much land. He proposed such a substantial reduction that the ambition to produce a new championship course could not have been realised, and the dream was dead.

Perhaps anticipating difficulties with this proposal the directors had not ignored the possibility of continuing to operate on the existing site. Critical to following this option was to secure as much of the course as possible against future residential development. The Board authorised the chairman, Mr. E.P. Taylor and his deputy Mr. A.B. Dawson, who was also the Borough Treasurer, to investigate possible solutions (Fig.57). The pair met Councillor Faulkner, a representative for the Ainsdale Ward, to discuss the Planning and Improvement Committee's provisional town plan, which scheduled much of the existing course for future building development. The strategy was to oppose the presentation of this plan to the Council and get it amended, if possible, to get the golf course zoned as white land, which would free it from the danger of development. With this threat removed, the value of the land would be considerably reduced. This campaign involved much lobbying and hard work. The Club drew on all its influence with the Council, and succeeded in persuading it to support the S&A case. This meant that the course was no longer designated as potential building land. With the threat to tenure removed, the Club was able think about a future on the existing course.

There had been little change to the Braid re-ordered course since the 1920s and in January 1946 the Board agreed to continue to function on this existing course, a plan which would satisfy '…the golfing requirements, maintain our existing clubhouse site and cost much less to develop.' The chairman and the secretary, Crewe Roden, advised by Ivor Newington, a solicitor and future captain, negotiated with the Estate for an extended lease. By March a new fourteen-year lease, for 148 acres had been agreed, with an annual rental of £265. The Club did accept, however, that when the old lease expired, the Estate had the right to re-possess land around the 12th and 13th holes, on six months notice, in order to allow further development along Ryder Crescent and the creation of Dunster Road (Fig.58).

58. The course during the 1937 Ryder Cup Match.
The triangle of holes comprising 'Tattenham Corner' is clearly visible. Note the remnants of field cops.

Anticipating that this land would be lost, new contracts were agreed with Steer for him to present a plan for course reconstruction. Work on staking out some new holes was commenced in the September.

The 12th green and the 13th tee formed the apex of the triangle at Tattenham Corner. These would be lost along with most of the fairways of these holes. The 11th hole, which formed the base of the triangle survived untouched. It was decided to retain the 12th tee and play this hole to the 13th green (Fig.59). To facilitate the construction of this replacement hole, a large and very tall sandhill had to be moved from the middle of the Tattenham Corner Triangle. From this new 12th hole the round continued on the old 14th hole, which became the new 13th (Fig.60). These alterations were not achieved without some alarms. After the new 12th fairway had been laid, a row of surveyor's poles appeared down its centre. It appears that there had been a surveying error and the hole had to be moved to fall within the agreed boundary. Having lost the 13th hole a further hole had to be created. It was decided to replace the existing 18th hole with two new holes. This involved absorbing the wild area at the south-west corner of the Club's land. The work was to be done by Club staff, using hired earthmoving equipment with one of the staff acting as foreman, under

59. New houses replaced the apex of the 'Tattenham Corner' triangle.

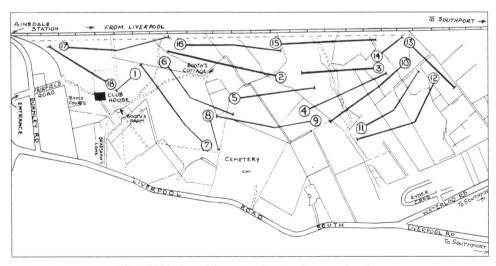

60. A 1952 plan of the course showing the re-construction.

85

61. Work on the new 17th green 1947.

Steer's supervision. The new 17th was a demanding 428 yards. It was a slight dog-leg, played from the present 18th tee, to a curving fairway that is now part of the practice ground. The green was tucked in the corner of the course near to the railway (Fig.61). For the 18th hole, an elevated tee was constructed behind this green to give a short par four of only 270 yards, the site for the green being that of the present 18th hole (Fig.62). Some additional land to achieve this change had been part of the Highway Department's depot. The Corporation rented it to the Club on a series of short leases at a nominal price. The abandoned 18th fairway became a conveniently sited, if small, practice area (Fig.63).

In addition to these major changes, there were modifications of existing holes. The 4th and 5th greens were both moved, thereby shortening the 4th by forty yards, the new green being cut into the slope of the hill, and adding approximately the same yardage to the 5th. It was 1949 before all eighteen holes of the new course could be played. In praising the greens in a 1948 article in *Golf Illustrated*, Jon Hope reported that J.A. Marshall, the greenkeeper, took: '…special pains to avoid leatherjackets and other evils' and that '…about 6 tons of compost go on each green every year and there is a plentiful supply of water laid on.' This is hardly the treatment recommended by contemporary consultants, although it is interesting to note that it was about this time that Leonard Crawley, the distinguished *Daily Telegraph* golf correspondent, judged the greens at S&A to be the best in the country.

After four years of negotiation the lease was again renewed in 1955, at an annual rental of £375. The urban net around the golf course was tightening and the fact that the Club had only secured another short lease, with an expiry date in 1975, made members of the Board uneasy. Some directors led by the chairman, Tom Barker, argued that the Club should attempt to purchase the land. He received strong support from his vice-chairman Ivor Newington. The third member of the trinity, which was to negotiate with the Estate on this possibility, was Tom Bunting, an estate agent. After preliminary interviews and correspondence with the two main beneficiaries of the Estate, Barker and Bunting went to London, in 1962, to meet Mr.

62. *Dunlop-Southport Tournament 1957.*
Flory van Donck driving from the elevated 18th tee.

Weld the chief trustee. The delegation had three options it wished to discuss with him. The first was the possibility of an extension of the lease; the second was the possibility of paying a premium to secure a three nines (999 years) lease; whilst the third, and most optimistic idea, was that the Club might be allowed to purchase the freehold of the course.

The delegation presented every argument it could marshal for the preservation of the course. Mr. Weld was told that over fifty of the members, who numbered over 500, were local juniors, and that the course was an

63. Centre – the abandoned fairway of the 18th 'Home' hole, at a right angle to it is the new 18th hole. The professional's shop can be seen alongside the clubhouse.

important 'open space' in a residential area. Although sympathetic to the Club's position, Mr. Weld told the delegation that the trustees were not interested in an extended lease, he explained that their aim was to realise the assets in the most profitable manner. He pointed out that the current value of the 139 acres, if planning permission for building were granted, would be something well in excess of £250,000. The delegation then posed the question what figure would he accept in cash for an outright purchase of the freehold, if planning permission was applied for and refused, and if the Club then guaranteed not to use the land for any other purpose than for golf? He suggested that the Club should make an offer, which he could put to his co-trustees and the beneficiaries. The pair then took the responsibility upon themselves to offer £20,000. Mr Weld promised to consider this offer, and added that in the event of a deal he would recommend that the Club should also purchase the freehold of the land on which the clubhouse was built, and also Booth's Farm, as the Estate would not wish to be left with any odd bits of land in the vicinity.

After further discussion the Estate forwarded a draft contract to the Club. A purchase price of £25,000 had been agreed, and there was also a clause stating that in the event of the development of the land for any purpose other than golf, the Club would sell the land back to the Estate for the same price. The Estate then made application to the Southport Corporation to develop the land for residential building purposes. For a while it looked as though the outcome might go its way. Speaking at Hesketh Golf Club's annual dinner, the Mayor seemed to indicate that the decision to grant planning permission had been made and that he was very pessimistic about the future of S&A. At this point the Board sought an interview with the Town Council's Planning and Improvement Committee to plead its case before a formal decision was made, and this was granted. Individual members of the Council were also lobbied on the issue, and this intense activity was rewarded when, at a meeting on the 27th January 1963 of the Town Planning Committee, an application for development was refused. This was probably the most important single incident in the history of S&A.

The way was open for a sale price to be negotiated with the Estate. The price finally agreed was £27,839, with a selling back price of £24,539 (Fig.64). To finance this purchase a loan was obtained which was supported by Certificates made out in units of twenty-five pounds, each carrying a rebate of a pound off subscriptions. All annual subscriptions were also raised by a third. On this occasion the members responded enthusiastically to the appeal and the amount required was quickly raised. At last, in 1964, the

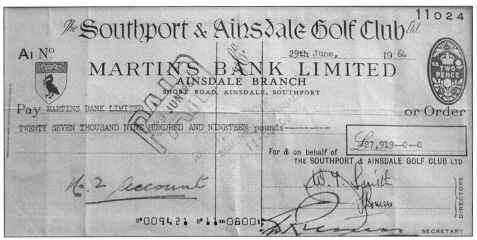

64. The cheque for the purchase of the course 1964.

Club could enjoy security of tenure. It held its own freehold, whilst Southport's other three major golf clubs would have to continue to pay rent to their landowner, the local Council, which had bought their courses from the landowners in the 1930s.

Small incremental changes to the course continued to be made. In 1964 as a result of 'pressure' from the houses in Dunster Road and Clovelly Drive the 12th hole was given a new green alongside the existing one. The legacy of this now departed green is still present. It was built on a bed of 'bluebilly' - sewage works residue. The presence of such nutrient enriched areas on the course is a recurring problem where soils and turf from old greens or tees have been dumped. The result is the growth of broad-leafed meadow grasses, rather than the fine leafed drought tolerant forms, which typify a links.

The Board recognised that the acquisition of additional land was not a realisable aim. Nevertheless the lack of a practice ground area was causing concern. Provision was restricted to the small area of abandoned fairway of the former 18th hole. This was seen not only as a handicap for the members but was also believed to be a disincentive for the playing of professional events at S&A. The Board commissioned Messrs Hawtree, eminent golf architects who included the Royal Birkdale course in their portfolio, to investigate the possibility of creating a practice ground at S&A. Such amenities are best located within the vicinity of the clubhouse, and this appears to have guided the thinking. In 1965 they produced a scheme that provided for a reversion to the former Braid designed 17th and 18th holes,

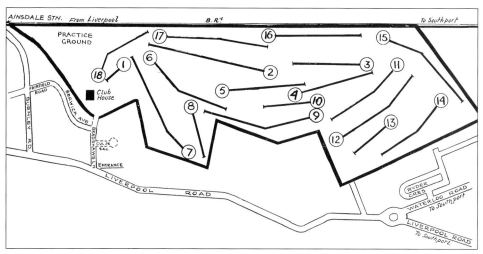

65. A 1975 plan of the course showing the introduction of two new short holes - the 10th and 13th.

with 'Heather' at 437 yards and 'Home' at 361. The loss of the 18th was compensated by the introduction of a new 160 yard short hole in the middle of the round – the 10th (Fig.65). Hawtree also proposed lengthening the 12th and 13th holes to incorporate into the course some land that had been left unused and thus vulnerable to developers. It was 1969 before the altered course came into play. The new practice ground, in the south-west corner of the course, was relatively small, and the lack of space dictated the need for discipline to be exercised by the users. To help in this, colour coded posts were erected and members were asked to practise from a post to one of a similar colour. More recently Health and Safety legislation has meant that players using the practice ground are required to adhere to a planned pattern of use. A risk assessment had to be made and a policy for usage is being developed and will need to be agreed with the local authority. Some form of supervision of the area may be necessary. Distance markers have been added to improve the quality of this facility, and an elevated pitching green, with inset bunkers, has been added.

J.J.F. Pennick, a leading golf course architect, was asked to look at holes nine to fifteen, in 1969. Not all of his recommendations were adopted, but it was decided to remove the short 15th hole and replace it with a new 13th. This was another short hole measuring 175 yards. The green was flanked by two clumps of trees and there was a pond beyond the green. With the removal of the short 15th some fifty yards were added to the old 14th to create the 342-yard long 15th.

91

Later, in 1986, the Club retained Donald Steel to survey the course and particularly to make recommendations for the 13th and 14th holes. A new elevated pear-shaped green was installed on the 13th and the spoil created was used to help form mounds to screen the property at the right of the 14th hole. This bank was landscaped in an attempt to give it the look of natural dunes. Blown sand from the coast road was used but also nutrient rich material that encouraged luxuriant green growth, including tall weeds, rather than brown wispy dune growth.

Further course modification came in 1999, when the Board approved the spending of £18,000 for a new green on the 3rd hole, on the site of the abandoned green of the old short 15th, and for moving the 4th tee back.

It was about this time that Gaunt & Marnoch were asked to draw plans for changes to the 7th, 8th & 9th. Their radical proposals, involving major earthworks, were not acceptable to the Club. 2001 saw plans for a new re-sited green for the 12th designed by Cameron Sinclair. Again the final decision was not to proceed.

Donald Steel produced a second comprehensive survey of the course in 2002. A major thrust of this report was to make suggestions on ways in which the course could be adapted to respond to the ever-increasing distances that new technology was allowing golfers to hit a golf ball. These proposals involved the removal of many old bunkers that no longer served their intended purpose and the creation of new bunkers sited to challenge the better golfers. This strategy of modifying the existing holes has been progressively implemented, and was described by the report's compilers as '...moving the furniture'.

Away from the concerns of course reconstruction, general course management and maintenance appeared to be going forward smoothly when disaster hit. Traffic on the course had increased enormously. By the mid 1990s, something in the order of 50,000 rounds a year were being played. This was a tenfold increase since 1950. Persistent heavy rain in the early part of 1995 resulted in several holes being flooded, and, in common with other clubs on the coast, the course was closed for a prolonged period (Fig.66). A long hot dry summer followed and subsequently a terrible scourge afflicted the fairways, particularly the 2nd, 6th and 17th. Much of the drought stressed grass was discoloured or dead. An urgent survey was commissioned from an agronomist. In order to protect the fairways, it was deemed necessary for golfers to carry and use small mats, which caused

66. The inundation 1995 – looking down the 2nd hole.

some to dub S&A - 'Southport and Axminster'. A trolley ban was introduced and an embargo put on accepting bookings from visitors. In the following year the greenkeeper wished to close the course in August and September to allow an over-seeding programme. This was the last straw for some of the members, who had had to endure a prolonged period of playing restrictions. Dissatisfaction bubbled over and a compromise was reached. Fourteen of the fairways were closed for re-seeding, but only one at a time. These areas were deemed ground under repair and shots had to be played off mats placed in the rough. Poor germination followed due to dry ground conditions, but, after further re-seeding and the introduction of a full irrigation system, the remedial action began to take effect enabling a return to normality. One legacy from the incident was the realization that the employment of mats during the winter months, when the grass is dormant, has a beneficial effect on the condition of the course in the early spring period, similarly with temporary prohibitions on the use of trolleys. Subsequently the improved condition of the course has drawn much praise from summer visitors. The other lesson learned was the importance of fairway irrigation.

In the early 1970s the Green Committee had wanted to follow the example being set by clubs throughout the country, who were installing irrigation systems. Previously the greenkeeper had got to manage with two portable pumps mounted on trailers, drawing water from the sixteen sleeper-lined wells on the course. Watering the greens would take four men all day, and it was argued that the use of hose pipes led to poor application of the water and encouraged the development of coarse grass. The membership backed the Board, voting for an irrigation scheme costing approximately £7,000. The well by the 18th green was enlarged to create a reservoir, and the system's specification required that the sprinklers should be able to water all the greens and tees in two nights. Installation was complete and the system ready for use by January 1972. Parts of this system were upgraded several times during the 1980s.

The large pond formed to serve as a reservoir proved to be a source of weakness. Despite several modifications of the intake, there was a persistent problem with sand getting into the system and clogging its smooth working. Scour by the sand in plastic pipes also led to leaks. Trespassing children playing in and around the pond eroded the banks and muddied the waters, thus exacerbating the problems. The Board decided to lease the fishing rights in the hope that this would introduce a stable body of anglers to help 'police' the area of the lake. A succession of groups took the lease, but in 1996 it was finally decided to discontinue this initiative, as it was not seen to be serving its original purposes. The lake is no longer used as part of the irrigation system and the area has been opened up and landscaped and has become a feature overlooked from the dining room, there is, however, a possibility that it may be filled in or that the fish are removed to deter unauthorised anglers.

After the experience of 1995, it was decided to extend irrigation to some of the fairways in a scheme costing over £200,000. A levy of £420 per head payable over a five-year period was proposed. The scheme was installed in 1998. In order to avoid the problems of sand in the system, water was extracted from underground using a well point system, and a large covered storage tank was built behind the greenkeeper's building. The water is metered and the Club is only able to pump up to an annual allowed figure, for which an extraction fee has to be paid.

The Club's *Newsletter No.1*, in 1969, had announced a winter tree-planting programme and referred to: 'The natural absence of trees on our windswept links', but by the 1990s the era of enthusiastic tree planting had passed. A sub-committee to oversee course development was convened in 1992. One of its early concerns was woodland management. The local clubs were removing alien tree species from the dune lands and attempting to restore the 'links' look. This clearance was not merely aesthetic, it also served a practical purpose as the root systems and physical presence of trees growing close to tees and greens denied them water, light and air and had an adverse effect on their well-being, as did the fall of deciduous leaves. At S&A, it was particularly white poplar ('Lancashire weed') that was being removed. In addition to damaging the course, this specie was causing problems at the boundaries of the course, where its shallow far-spreading roots were invading adjoining properties and threatening the drains. Although there was still a tree fund in the budget and 200 trees were planted in 1992, these consisted mainly of pines planted for screening on the course boundaries. The felling of mature trees is always emotive and there was opposition from some members. Such was the sensitivity on this issue that all decisions on woodland management had to go to the Board. Trees scheduled for removal were first identified with a paint mark to allow members to register their views.

Less problematic than woodland clearance was the partnership forged with the Sefton Coast Life Project, to manage the rough. Gorse and heather were protected and willow scrub removed. After heather had been cut back, the 'brashings' were used in an attempt to colonize other areas of the course. The dune heath at S&A accounted for a quarter of the surviving dune heath in Sefton; whilst the area of heather dominated dune heath was of national significance. Indeed, S&A contains an important population of rare grey hair grass, largely on the left of the 7th hole. It seems that S&A is the only site where in can be found on the west coast of Britain.

Without management, trees such as the white poplar would smother the gorse and heather. Members were still concerned, however, about the removal of trees and the implications for golf of the designation of the course as a Site of Special Scientific Interest (SSSI 1). An Open Forum in 1997 helped members to better understand the issues and how restoring the dunes would open up aspects of rolling dunes and be to the benefit of the indigenous wildlife. As a result the Club received a 'Countryside Stewardship Grant' from Defra (the Department of the Environment, Farming and Rural Affairs), which was spread over ten years. This provided financial support for the clearing of scrub, poplars, invasive woodland and other tree problems. It was recognized that woodland should be retained to screen along the boundaries and on some holes, act as features in the landscape, and to provide a habitat for birds and mammals. The programme included the planting, in 1999, of a broad band of holly, birch, rosa rugosa and Corsican pines on the bank by the cemetery. The latter were chosen in an attempt to encourage red squirrels. To this end, under a new Sefton Coast Woodland Plan, the favoured balance is for planting pine with only about ten per cent broad-leafed content. Tree clearance continued and in 1999 sycamores were removed from the back of the 16th green and from behind the 8th green in 2004. Dr. Brian Gill, a biologist, was asked to '...take responsibility for all ecological matters on the course', and he later became chairman of the Green Committee. Donald Steel's report in 2002 gave strong support for the policy of removing deciduous trees from within the golf course and concentrating tree planting on the boundaries to '...fulfil an important screening and safety role.' The Club's consultant ecologist recommends planting informal hedges of mixed thorns on some of the boundaries.

Rabbits on the course continued to be a problem and gas eradication measures were regularly employed, followed by control using ferrets. The use of gas was frowned upon by environmentalists because of its indiscriminate impact on wildlife other than rabbits, but it was judged to be a necessary measure. Environmental sensitivity now dictates that it is no longer used.

67. The greenkeeping staff 2005.
From the left: Steven Haliwell, John Reynolds, Keith Mercer, Michael Mercer, John Taylor and Tony Rimmer.

The head greenkeeper is always an employee of critical importance to a golf club and Michael Mercer took the post in 1984. The old shed was no longer deemed to be adequate for the housing and maintenance of the increasing collection of expensive equipment, and certainly failed to meet the statutory requirements in respect of accommodation for the six full-time staff (Fig.67). It was replaced at a cost of more than £80,000 in 1996.

The efforts of the greenkeepers continued to be supplemented by work provided by the artisans. They make a particularly valuable contribution to the labour-intensive tasks of divoting and path maintenance. Working on the course had become a more popular duty than acting as marshals in an attempt to reduce trespass and vandalism. The artisan team to play in a match against the Club scratch team in 1948 consisted of ten players with handicaps between two and seven. At the top of this team Percy Halsall (2), the brother of Birkdale's long-serving professional Bobby Halsall, beat Tom Hiley 1 up. In the same year he won the first post-war North of England Artisan Golf Championship, which was played at S&A. In 1956 the artisans were able to improve their club room, the Board chairman obtained a further building for them, which they had to transport and erect, next to their existing structure. The 1970s saw this replaced by a sectional concrete building. These improvements have helped to ensure the development of the artisans as an active golfing and social unit.

Chapter Five

THE CLUB AND THE CLUBHOUSE

*S&A members are friendly. It is a fine Club that can afford the members,
rather than a group of members that can afford the Club.*
The President of the English Golf Union 1987

Following the removal of the initial post-war threat to the future of the course, the security of extended tenure encouraged further development of the clubhouse. At a Board meeting in November 1946 Mr. Len Birkett, the immediate past captain, offered to obtain a sectional wooden building, formerly part of the Flotilla Club, for use as a billiard room annexe. (The Flotilla Club was a Liverpool club for sailors and Birkett was its honorary secretary. Birkett is probably best remembered for the refreshing non-alcoholic drink which he invented, which still bears his name and is a standard order in the bars of all the local golf clubs.) At this period there was only one billiard table in the clubhouse and it was situated in the main lounge. Birkett's offer was accepted and the annexe erected at the rear of the clubhouse, with access from the main lounge. This area later became the site of the dining room. A second billiard table was purchased and in September 1947 the first final of the snooker competition was held, followed by a hot-pot supper. Snooker became a more important part of the social life of the Club, and in 1952 a winter league was established and matches with other clubs followed. An exhibition match involving John Spencer, a leading professional, was played in 1970. A new brick-built snooker room, to accommodate two tables and served by a small adjacent bar, was built at the north-east end of the clubhouse in 1980. It was only then that the annual snooker trophy – the Andy Lancaster Trophy - was introduced in 1982.

Relatively small incremental improvements to the clubhouse, rather than comprehensive reconstruction schemes, were the order of the day. In 1956 it was realised that direct access to the changing room through a new external door at the end of the verandah would allow the entrance hall to be upgraded. There was pressure from some members for the provision of a mixed lounge. At an EGM of the ladies' section, they gave unanimous support for such a scheme but a majority of those present also voted against a proposal to use the ladies' lounge for this purpose on certain evenings. The enclosing of the central portion of the verandah to create a mixed

68. The mixed lounge from the 18th fairway.
The tall chimney of the Ainsdale Laundry was a striking landmark.

lounge was completed in 1959 (Fig.68). Although enjoying magnificent views, this facility does not appear to have enjoyed universal acclaim. Its location, as an extension of the men's lounge, was fraught with problems. Ladies had '...no right of access to, or egress from the mixed lounge through the gentlemen's lounge.' Consequently it was difficult for unaccompanied ladies to place an order at the bar. At an appointed time in the evening heavy curtains were drawn to close it off (Fig.69).

In the late 1970s a major re-development of the clubhouse was considered but not carried forward; piecemeal development continued. The wooden billiard annexe was replaced by a brick-built dining room. Around 1980 the men's toilets and shower room were re-furbished. It was the 1990s before the lockers were upgraded, but this was done within the existing locker room.

As S&A approached its centenary year there was a move to undertake a fundamental review of the clubhouse and its facilities, with a view to meeting the perceived needs of the twenty-first century. A Clubhouse Development Committee, with co-opted members with relevant expertise, was convened.

99

69. The mixed lounge on a Sunday morning. Note the service bar.

Its chairman, Keith Hendrick, put its proposals to an Extraordinary General Meeting of the Club in November 2003 and a majority of those who voted supported the scheme.

The major problem identified appeared to be the inadequacy of the existing locker rooms. Additionally there was no spike bar; there was a centrally located casual bar, but it had no direct external access. Solutions to these problems did not appear to be available within the confines of the existing eighty-years-old building. Its location on the top of a hill complicated the possibilities. Lower down the slope of the mound was the professional's shop. This detached building stood in the way of northern expansion of the clubhouse, and also suffered from the inferior quality of its construction in 1925. The plan involved its demolition and the excavation of the mound between it and the clubhouse. Thus the way was cleared for a two-storey extension to the existing building. The extension is slightly lower than the original clubhouse, but sympathetically designed in its 'bungalow style' (Fig.70). It provided space for new, larger male and female locker rooms, a replacement shop for the professional and an open plan office for the secretariat (Fig.71). The central bar and lounge areas have been

70. The clubhouse with the extension 2005.

71. The secretariat 2005: from the left: Simon Aplin, Elaine Power, and Carol Birrell, the Club Secretary.

refurbished and the casual bar extended to give external access from the terrace in front of the clubhouse, thus creating a genuine spike bar. The former ladies' lounge, locker room and the Ryder Room have been combined to provide a vastly bigger dining room. Unlike the old dining room, diners now have views of the course and the lake. The scheme also provides both access and facilities for the disabled.

To finance the estimated £867,000 for the scheme, an annual supplement on the subscriptions was imposed for fifteen years. Loan notes, which offered discounts on subscriptions, proportionate to the amount invested, were also available. The Committee set itself the target of having the work completed within twelve months. As with many schemes to extend existing clubhouses, the project was not without unanticipated construction problems. Nevertheless the target date was achieved. It was, however, a close run thing - on Friday 17th December 2004, carpet fitters and furnishers were desperately adding the final touches. On the following evening it was Captain Graham Fisher's 'Final Fling'. After having had to cope with the inconveniences of construction, throughout his year in office, it was appropriate that he should host the first function in the 'new' clubhouse. Richard Cole-Hamilton, the Captain of the R&A, performed the official opening, on the 5th March 2005 (Fig.72). In his complimentary comments on the Club, the course and the clubhouse, he recalled that his previous visit to S&A had been as an undergraduate with a Cambridge University team in 1956.

Throughout the last half-century efforts were made to mount social events, which would attract members to use the clubhouse. Race nights had a strong appeal to members for a number of years and a profit of about £200 was regularly made on such evenings. Commercially sponsored golf films, which could be borrowed free of charge, were also popular in the 1960s and 1970s. On the first Saturday of each month the gentlemen's lounge, now free of the snooker table, was used for a dance social, with music provided by a three-piece band. The clubhouse contains a piano and amplification equipment for use on social occasions. The New Year's Eve party was so popular that it was over-subscribed even when the limit was raised to 240. Bonfire night and family Christmas parties were also an attraction. Particularly popular was the annual festive season visit by Stackstead Brass Band, from East Lancashire. The Club resisted installing a television set until 1964. However, it was the influence of television in the home, changes in social patterns, and a new attitude toward drinking and driving that led S&A to share the fate of the majority of golf clubs in failing to attract its members to use the clubhouse socially on a regular basis. In 1999 a group

72. Richard Cole-Hamilton, the Captain of the R&A, opening the clubhouse extension 5th March 2005. From left: Errol Cheesman (Captain), Keith Hendrick, Linda Nolte (Lady Captain), Cole-Hamilton and Paul Gwynne.

of younger members were asked to form a committee to advise the Social Committee on how their generation might be encouraged to make greater use of the clubhouse and thus help increase turnover.

Bridge playing has not seemed to play as big a role as appears to be the case at other local golf clubs. Nevertheless, in 1963 the Captain announced what he described as '...something unique in this Club, the winning of the Southport Bridge League Tournament', a success that was repeated in the following year.

Celebration dinners were held in the clubhouse to mark milestones in the golfing careers of the Club's individual golfing giants (Fig.73). A triple celebration dinner was held in 1973 to mark David Marsh's captaincy of the Walker Cup team, Dixon Rawlinson's captaincy of the Lancashire county team, and Tom Bunting's year as President of the Lancashire Union of Golf Clubs. The Annual dinner had long since outgrown the clubhouse, its popularity demanding a venue that could accommodate over 200 diners. It has continued to be held at the Prince of Wales Hotel, and for a period under canvas at the Tree Tops Hotel, Woodvale. The Prince of Wales and the Royal Clifton hotels have been the venues for the annual dinner dance.

73. Dinner to celebrate Geoff Roberts winning the English Amateur Championship 1951.

1968 saw the beginnings of a new tradition at the incoming captain's New Year's Day drive in. From this time the caddies of some of the captains appeared on the first tee in fancy dress. Captains followed their example and soon the event had become a theatrical 'production number'. In 1977 the kilted John Graham was carried to the tee on a stretcher accompanied by a white-coated doctor and medical orderlies. The content of the drip feed bottle was more S&A than National Health. The theme of these events began to reflect the captain's profession or hobby. Vernon Cubbon arrived at the tee concealed in a giant mobile mixing bowl from which he emerged dressed as a master baker, and Peter Lennon popped out of a packing case, unloaded from a container by a fork-lift truck. The casts involved became larger; Michael Edwards had a colourful troupe of Irish Leprechauns to support him, cueist Peter Wilding's aides were dressed as snooker balls, whilst Stan Jackson and his fly-fishers landed an extraordinary catch. Possibly the most spectacular event was that of building inspector David Ball, whose team arrived at the tee, erected a scaffold tower, from the top of which his inaugural drive was then successfully struck (Fig.74).

S&A captains and past captains have been enthusiastic supporters of the Liverpool Society of Golf Club Captains (Fig.75). The Society's first annual meeting following the Second World War was held at S&A in 1948. The Club has supplied the Society, which is made up by the captains and past captains of twenty-seven Merseyside clubs, with two of its captains – Tom Barker in 1957, and Stan Dickinson in 1982. The Club has also provided competition winners. The Annual Competition was won by George Butler in 1956, H. Cameron Booth in 1960, Eddie Sims in 1979 and David Ball in 1999; whilst Ivor Newington (1952) and David Marsh (1977) won the Scratch Prize. John Gregory won the Spaven Trophy for veterans, in 1978, the first year it was awarded, a victory repeated by Peter Lennon in 2001. S&A members have also been successful in the annual three-day Autumn meeting. John Walker won the

74. David Ball gets to the top;
the Captain's New Year's Day drive-in 1996.

individual award – the John Benstead Trophy – in 1995, a feat repeated by Alan Ravey in 2005. Alan, along with Graham Fisher, Chris Walker and Eddie Williams also won the team prize – the Jack Stanway Johnson Trophy.

Officers serving at RAF Woodvale were able to enjoy a group membership at S&A. In a reciprocal gesture, Club members were invited to share in social occasions in the mess at Woodvale. To mark the special relationship, members of the mess presented a trophy to the Club, an event celebrated in spectacular fashion by a fly-past of training aircraft (Fig.76). The airfield was also the source of 'spoil', which was used in the periodic course alterations. Thus soil from the old Freshfield Golf Club course now forms part of S&A.

Through the war years there had been a regular recruitment of Merseyside Catholic priests into the Club and by the early 1960s the group, which had formerly played at West Derby, had grown to over forty in number. The priests arranged their own competitions, supervised their own handicaps and played an annual fixture against the rest of the Club. The arrangements normally worked smoothly although in 1972 Father Finn, the organiser, was

75. Captain and past captains 2005. Seated from the left: Mike Edwards (1983), Eddie Williams (1981), Vernon Cubbon (1979), John Walker (1972), The Captain - Errol Cheesman, Dr David Marsh (1967), John Graham (1977), Bert Beddows (1984), Roger Backhouse (1985), Standing; Les Morgan (1998), Chris Walker (2002), Hugh Waterson (1991), Ian White (1992), Ron Draper (2000), Jim O'Rourke (1987), Graham Fisher (2004), David Ball (1996), Bill Whinnett (1997), Stan Jackson (1995), Alex Greaves (1988), George Thomas (2003), Alan Ravey (2001), Mike Attenborough (1999), Mike Bennett (1986), Peter Lennon (1989)

76. The presentation of the Woodvale Trophy marked by a fly-past 1985.
From the left: Captain Roger Backhouse, Ron Mottishead (winner) and Squadron Leader Mike Connell.

'...asked to identify and admonish those priests whose habit it is to interrupt their round of golf and undertake refreshment in one of the shelters on the course.' It appears that when they emerged some would cut in front of the ladies! By the end of the century, the number of priests had fallen to twenty, half of whom were veteran members.

Although the scratch competitions loomed large in S&A's golfing calendar, there was also a good number of handicap competitions allowing those of more modest attainment to share the gold paint of the honours boards. The life-blood of the Club is the regular social/competitive golf enjoyed by the members. From 1948 the Club organised an official Sunday morning league. The format was to play four-ball golf, with a regular partner, on a points basis. After a successful first year the scheme was expanded to encompass two leagues, then three. With fourteen pairs in each league, eighty-four members were regularly involved. It was claimed that these

Sunday morning games provided excellent training for the younger players. The Winter League continues to be an important feature of Club golf, and has been supplemented by the Sunday Morning Winter Knockout. Centenary Captain Paul Gwynne indicated his readiness for this golfing challenge by winning this Winter League in 2004, with his partner Chris Walker. S&A has also experienced its share of unusual golfing occurrences. In May 1953 four members were playing in a social four-ball match. After their blind second shots on the 3rd hole, they found three of the four balls '…touching and forming a clover leaf shape on the green.' Fifty years later, the October Monthly Medal produced another extraordinary event, three members scored maiden aces at the 153-yard 8th hole. Publicity in the national press failed to reveal a similar achievement elsewhere.

In addition to the outstanding record of the S&A scratch teams, the Club has also enjoyed a number of 'social' fixtures. Such games were played with Wigan, West Derby and Hillside. Indeed, at least one match with Hillside was played on the basis of sixty-a-side. Oddly it was only recently that regular fixtures with the Club's nearest neighbour have been formalised. A scratch team fixture with another neighbour, Hesketh, has become a social captain's match. Fixtures with Ilkley Golf Club provided a highly sociable outing, as did exchange golfing days with the Sandiway and Pleasington clubs. A reciprocal golf exchange arrangement has now been made with the Wallasey club.

During the war, tourism to Ireland had all but disappeared, and in an effort to revive it the Irish Tourist Board promoted a sporting festival -'An Tostal' – in 1954. The Board sponsored visits from teams across a range of sports and the personal links of some S&A members led to the Club being invited to send a team to play a match with Castletroy Golf Club in Limerick. There might have been an element of exaggeration in accounts of the party that followed, although Irish sporting hospitality is the stuff of legends. In the following year, members of the Castletroy Club made a return visit to S&A, which was linked with an outing to the Grand National.

As an alternative to promoting professional golf, after its withdrawal from the Dunlop-Southport tournament, the Southport Corporation decided to mount an annual golf week for amateurs. It was an event designed to encourage visitors to take a holiday in the town and was held in the week after the Flower Show. A varied programme of competitions was offered on the town's four major courses; a club received twenty-five pounds from the Corporation for hosting one of the events. The week was concluded by a presentation dance at the Floral Hall. As an incentive to competitors they were issued with tickets to play a practice round on the courses where they were due to compete.

The event, which was held for the first time in 1949, proved to be very popular, particularly with local golfers. As the fundamental purpose of the golf week was to attract visitors to the town, the Corporation officials attempted to adjust the regulations to encourage their participation. Practice round concessions for local players were reduced, and then withdrawn, and some of the prizes were restricted to visitors. The week continued to be very popular, but local players were still the principal supporters. Despite the adjustments to the regulations, the basic attraction remained - the opportunity for cheap competitive golf on the town's leading courses. The clubs lost their enthusiasm for the event and the Corporation decided to discontinue it in 1957. In 2005, the Club successfully introduced its own income generating three-day golf festival.

There was a welcome legacy for S&A from the Southport Golf Week. The prize in the principal men's competition had been a handsome silver cup, which had German origins and apparently had come into the Corporation's hands during the war. The Club came to an agreement with the Corporation to continue to organise an eighteen-hole handicap competition annually, with the cup as the trophy. This Southport Bowl remained the property of the authority, and the Club was responsible for the organisation and for providing prizes. This was the status of the event up to 1977, at which time sixteen of the first twenty-eight winners had been members of S&A. The competition had lost its meaning and it was decided to fundamentally change the nature of the event. It became an important thirty-six-hole open scratch competition, and has since taken its place on the regional amateur circuit as a Mitsushiba Northern Order of Merit event, and is now known as the Southport and Ainsdale Bowl.

As the number of active retired members in golf clubs increased, a new phenomenon occurred – the emergence of formally organised matches for senior members. At S&A, what was described as an '…unofficial match for older members' was played with West Lancs in 1976. The team, raised by Bill Almond, also played against the ladies. This initiative soon developed into an officially approved veterans' team with regular matches for members over the age of fifty-five. Stan Wagstaff was the early organiser, and in 1977 the Board allowed the courtesy of the course to be extended to members of the visiting teams. It was ruled that players had to be over sixty-years-old and retired. In recent years Terry Kershaw has been the organiser, arranging matches with eight local clubs.

Veterans, who met set membership criteria, were allowed reduced rates of subscription, but changing social, demographic and economic considerations led to the partial withdrawal of this concession. Along with almost every other golf club the age profile at S&A revealed a significant bulge of members between the ages of fifty and seventy. Faced with this imbalance the Board decided that, when there were opportunities to recruit new members, 'emphasis' would be on the under fifties.

S&A has been particularly successful in recruiting youngsters. In 1948 there were only fifteen junior members and membership was opened up to include boys who did not have family associations with the Club. Amazingly a photograph of a group of twelve junior members of this generation includes two future captains of the Royal and Ancient Golf Club of St Andrews (Fig.77). The Board set a membership limit of thirty boys and appointed a junior organiser to be responsible for this section. Those undertaking these duties included Sam Robinson and Dixon Rawlinson. By 1960 junior membership was almost fifty. The Club, later assisted by the Golf Foundation, paid the professional to provide free lessons for juniors during the summer holidays (Fig.78). When he retired in 1975 Jack McLachlan had a class of about thirty every Saturday morning. The total number of junior members had risen to over eighty by 1984. The regard that some S&A members have for the juniors was demonstrated when, in 1996, one donated £600 to support junior golf in the Club. Peter Lennon, who had taken over from Stan Wagstaff, was the organiser about this time; Neil Leadbetter, Phil Towndrow and Steve Tremarco followed him. The Club undertook an analysis in 1999 to try to establish what were the membership implications of having such a large junior section. In 1993 there had been seventy-five junior members. By 1999, thirty-three of this cohort had formally resigned, eight had gone missing, eight were still juniors, but sixteen were colts and ten had become full members. This was a retention rate of forty-five per cent. Clearly this had important implications for the future of the Club. It was decided that a limit of sixty should be placed on the membership of the junior section, and an attempt made to ensure that membership was confined to enthusiastic, active golfers who knew how to conduct themselves on the course and off it. The assistance of senior members who might give them guidance on a day-to-day basis was sought, and members of the Club's scratch team volunteered to assist, acting not only as mentors in matters of technique, but also in the vitally important areas of etiquette and standards. In 2004 the junior organiser, Steve Tremarco, reported that there were fifty-six junior members, '…considerably more than the national golf club average.'

77. Juniors 1948. Back row, from the left: Nial Meredith, John Eccles, nk, nk,
Leyland Haughton, nk, Peter Turton, Ian Jeffrey, Peter Marsh, David Marsh*, Gordon Jeffrey*, Graham
Hayes, James Moore (S&A Captain), and Paul Carter. (* Future captains of the R&A.)

A category of Colt membership, with a reduced membership fee for those between eighteen and twenty-four years of age, was introduced in 1947. The impact of these generations of S&A youngsters has been remarkable. Some enjoyed outstanding amateur golfing careers; a few went on to become professional golfers, whilst many became good club members. At least two, John Graham and Roger Basford, were later appointed golf club secretaries; whilst Donald Holmes, a retired doctor, after being a Dorset county player, became president of both Dorset and South Western Counties and is the organiser of the European Seniors Team Championship. Many former colts went on to distinguish themselves in their professions. These include Nial Meredith, a competent golfer, who took holy orders, Ken Hulme, a single figure golfer who became the head of GCHQ, the heart of the nation's world-wide electronic surveillance, and Peter Brunt, who is the Queen's physician in Scotland. Later, Brendan Barber, a single figure golfer who won the Blackburn Holden Trophy in 1967, became the General Secretary of the Trade Unions Congress.

It is interesting to note the changes that had occurred in the areas from which the Club draws its male playing members. By the end of the twentieth century, the distribution reflected the rapid development of housing post 1960 in Ainsdale and Formby. The largest single locations were Ainsdale itself with 106 members and neighbouring Formby, including Freshfield, with eighty-two. Birkdale was not far behind being the home of seventy-four members; whilst there were only forty-two from Southport. The traditional links with Liverpool (nineteen) and the intermediate stops along the railway line (twenty-three) were still well represented. Scattered across south-west Lancashire from St Helens, through Ormskirk and Burscough, to Preston were another forty-nine members; whilst there were single members living in Bolton, Wigan and on the Wirral. This distribution points to a predominantly local membership, with the majority enjoying easy access to the course. Approximately half of the current 600 playing members are full seven day members.

Caddies were still a feature of club life after the war. A new caddiemaster was appointed in 1945 and the charge for junior caddies was set at half a crown (12.5p), whilst for a senior caddie the charge was three shillings and sixpence (17.5p). Members were asked not to give more than an additional sixpence (2.5p) as a tip. What were originally described as 'auto-caddies' (trolleys) were introduced in 1948. The Club made an annual charge for their storage and bought six to be hired out. Members had occasion to complain when they discovered that the professional had hired out their personal trolleys! The new devices did not immediately replace caddies and in 1967 a new caddiemaster was appointed. He stayed at S&A for over a decade and the old wooden caddies' stand, near the first tee, was replaced by a pre-cast concrete structure. The caddies were principally schoolboys. One prospective junior member of the Club was rejected because he wouldn't give up his role as a caddie. By 1976 the caddiemaster advised the Club that one pound was a reasonable rate for a round, but the Board decided that it had become impracticable for it to attempt to enforce a standard fee.

Members who had bought one of the narrow wheeled trolleys had to replace them, or fit broad wheels, when the earlier versions were banned from the course in 1979. In the early 1990s, the Board wanted motorised buggies to be allowed for a trial period on the course. They had proved to be a profitable source of revenue at several clubs. Opposition came, however, from the members at the AGM and the facility was restricted to those with confirmed medical problems. Time has moved on and the Club now has a small fleet of buggies available for hire.

Board minutes reveal occasional problems with some of the Club's neighbours. At the north end of the course some properties suffered from wardly struck balls; at the south end vandalism, associated with the pond, spilled over to surrounding property; whilst to the west, balls, were, it seems, being maliciously driven from the practice ground and striking the school, across the railway line. Members also experienced problems with another neighbour – Birkdale Cemetery. On seeing his ball fly out of bounds and ricochet amongst the gravestones, one member would comment 'Not lost but gone before.' The headstone of Bruce Naylor, a former member of the scratch team buried there, carries the inscription: 'Finally, a decent lie on the ninth.'

78. Professional Jack McLachlan adjusting Tony Rodwell's grip. Back row from the left: nk, Jill Basford, Shirley Almond, nk, nk, nk, nk, Roger Basford, Lionel Barham, nk, nk. c.1956.

Chapter Six

LADIES' GOLF AT S&A
Dorothy Ritchie

You women want equality, but you'll never get it because women are inferior to men in all sorts of ways; physically, intellectually and morally. There are exceptions, but on the whole women are inferior to men.
Severiano Ballesteros **The Daily Telegraph** *1996*

With the coming of World War II, golf slipped down the order of the ladies' priorities. It was March 1940, however, before the Board recognized that members serving in the Forces, who were exempted from paying fees, might include ladies. Normal club activities were suspended: competitions were cancelled, handicaps were frozen, and golf was confined to friendly games. Lady captains were not appointed, annual meetings not held and the existing committee remained in office. Emphasis was on assisting the war effort, and the ladies decided to support the Mayor's appeal to provide 'comforts' for Southport servicemen. Thursday afternoons saw members coming together in knitting and sewing circles. Money was raised through bridge drives and from a levy on golf games. Volunteers were recruited to staff a canteen at a relief camp in Maghull for the victims of the air raids on Liverpool. Later, social events to raise money for parcels for prisoners of war replaced the production of comforts. The ladies also supported the work of the Flotilla Club, a naval social club in Liverpool (Fig.79). It seems that an RAF plane crashed on the course in 1944 and in a brave, but vain, attempt to save the pilot from the burning wreckage, Mrs. E.A. (May) Smith, a future lady captain, received burns. Competitions were restored in 1943, but were limited to nine holes; an AGM was held in 1944, and a lady captain elected in 1945.

S&A's most distinguished lady golfer was undoubtedly Marjorie Barron. Although her international career had started in 1929, many of Marjorie's major successes were achieved after the war. At national level she won the Welsh Championship in 1947, 1957 and 1960, whilst she was runner-up in 1948 and 1956 (Fig.80). Normally good on the greens, Marjorie was having problems with putting during the 1956 semi-final and was five down on the 11th green. Her opponent, who knew Marjorie and her game well, pointed out what she believed was wrong. Her advice was so effective that Marjorie went on to win on the 19th.

79. Raising funds for the Flotilla Club 1942. Two sailors can be seen on the putting green.
Fashionable wartime turbans are in evidence, including one worn by Marjorie Wren, standing sixth from the right

At international level she represented Wales regularly between 1947 and 1963. A strong, independently minded woman, Marjorie was officially reprimanded for wearing trousers at Royal Porthcawl in the home internationals of 1958 (Fig.81). She was a stalwart of the Lancashire county team between 1953 and 1964, and, although she was never the Lancashire County Champion, she did go on to win the county veterans' title five times, and played many times for the Lancashire veterans' team. Her record of success in club trophies might not look impressive; she won the Match-Play Championship once and the Captain's Prize three times. It must be remembered, however, that she also won or tied for the Scratch Trophy in seventeen of the years between 1951 and 1977, including the record low score of 70.

Following her third success in the Welsh Championship in 1960, the Club recognised her outstanding golfing achievements and made her its first honorary life associate member. Her standing in golf was such that a page was devoted to her in Enid Wilson's *A Gallery of Women Golfers*. The author, an outstanding golfer who became the pre-eminent contemporary writer on ladies' golf, identified the running short approach with a straight-faced club as a shot Marjorie played well (Fig.82). She noted that Marjorie

115

80. Marjorie Barron with the Welsh Ladies' Championship Trophy 1947.

81. Marjorie Barron wearing trousers whilst playing during the home internationals at Royal Porthcawl in 1958.

eschewed the favoured aerial route, and '…tickles the ball up to the pin with a four or five iron…laying it dead.' Writing in *Golf Illustrated* she described Marjorie as having '…no pretensions to being a stylish swinger and she comes onto the ball with all the force she can muster.' She went on to suggest that: 'Like many other big and powerful people she putts well.'

When she died in 1982, the Lady Captain, June Gwynne, told members at the AGM that Marjorie was: 'The greatest lady golfer that the club has ever known, probably best described as a law unto herself.' Fellow international Pat Roberts MBE, who along with Marjorie dominated the Welsh Ladies' Championship for a period, winning it four times and being runner-up on six occasions, and who after a distinguished playing career served the Welsh Union as its president, chairman and secretary, still recalls Marjorie with great affection, describing her as '…a kind person who was a generous and pleasant opponent.'

In the early 1950s S&A won the County Scratch Shield and Marjorie Barron was joined in the Lancashire county team by a number of other S&A

116

members. Alison Reece, a member from the West Derby Club who joined S&A in 1949, played between 1953 and 1958. She also won the Lady Derby Challenge Cup in 1964: this competition involved a full week's play, with qualifying rounds and a knockout stage. Partnered by Sadie Smith, the Lady Captain, Alison was to lose in the final of the Northern Counties Foursome Competition to Royal Birkdale's illustrious international Bunty Stephens and her Lancashire county player partner, in 1953. At S&A she won the Scratch Trophy on six occasions, her best winning score being 74. Like Marjorie Barron she later had a distinguished playing record in representative veterans' golf, both became Lancashire champions but, unlike Marjorie, Alison, who became a member of Formby Ladies,

82. Marjorie Barron practising one of her favourite short running approach shots.

undertook a significant role in golf administration. She served as county secretary, captain and president, and was a committee member of ELGA. She was later to captain the Lancashire veterans, and became the association's president. Another S&A member, Kath Gregory, was to follow her in these two offices in 1981 and 1994.

A third S&A star of the post-war era was Eve Shand. She won the Scratch Trophy on four occasions, her best winning score being a 72 in 1965. Along with Marjorie and Alison she was a member of the Lancashire county team that won the Northern Counties Championship at S&A in 1958 (Fig.83). The same three successfully represented S&A in the scratch competition for the Lancashire Inter-Club Shield which was won by a clear nine strokes in appalling weather at St Anne's Old Links in 1964. Eve Shand was runner-up in the Lancashire Championship twice and lost in the semi-final on three occasions. She did however win the Carr Gold Medal in 1955 and 1960, for achieving the lowest qualifying round. Eve reached the last eight of the

*83. Lancashire Team c.1958. Back row from the left: Alison Reece (S&A),
Ruth Ferguson, Marjorie Barron (S&A), Sue Ashworth, Joan Morland, Ann Irvin,
Elsie Corlett, Ann Howard, and Eve Shand (S&A).*

English Close Championship in 1960. Two years previously, when the championship was played at Formby, she possibly set a record when it took her over half an hour to play one hole. With the score level after eighteen holes the match had to continue on the nineteenth. When the players arrived at the 1st green they found that the hole was under water following an earlier short storm. The caddie was dispatched to the clubhouse for advice. The greenkeepers had gone home and their shed was locked. The players had to wait until a key could be found and brooms brought out to clear the water. Eve apparently survived the wait best and won the hole and the match. Lady Captain in 1965, she was the fun loving joker in the pack. A member of the famous Shand family this socialite's reputation at S&A rested almost as much on the luxury cars that she drove, as it did on her excellence as a golfer.

84.Southport Golf Week 1954. A quartette of S&A ladies in the centre of the group on the 1st tee at Hillside. Fourth from the left Marjorie Wren, to her right Maimie Pollard, May Wilson, and Ida Shaw.

Miss A. Phillips and Liz Horrocks also achieved county honours, in this golden era of ladies' golf at S&A. They joined Marjorie, Alison and Eve in the Lancashire team that won the Northern Championship at Silloth in 1954. In addition, May Wilson and Mamie Pollard won the Lancashire Hilda Leggart Foursomes Trophy, in its inaugural year, in 1952. Not surprisingly, S&A ladies were also successful competitors in the Southport Golf Week, providing the winner of the Southport Bowl on numerous occasions (Fig.84).

A group of S&A past captains were amongst the founder members of the Liverpool Society of Lady Golf Captains, Alison Reece being asked to take the chair at the inaugural meeting in 1959. Alison won the silver handicap prize at the Society's Summer Meeting in 1976. Judy Bunting was captain of the Society in 1971, a position held by Janet Burley in 1983. Very sadly she died whilst in office. More recently, Dorothy Graham was captain in 1997. A number of Club members have been successful in Society events. In 1971 a team consisting of Dr. Anne Bateson, May Wilson and Sadie Smith won the

Hodson Trophy, a feat repeated in 1975, when Marjorie Wren replaced May Wilson. Marjorie also won the Society's Jackson Trophy, for the best nett score, at the advanced age of seventy-eight (Fig.85). Judy Bunting, who served on the executive committee of the LLCGA, won this trophy in the 1982 meeting. Flo Greaves won it again in 1991, and in the same year Dilys Rimmer and Dorothy Graham won the Jubilee Cup in the Society's Spring Meeting. An S&A team of Nancy Jenkins, Karen Buckels, Dorothy Graham, Dilys Rimmer, Josephine Cullen, Dorothy Ravey and Dian Albert won the Nicholson Trophy in the Spring Meeting, played at S&A, in 1996.

By 1969 the highly successful S&A scratch team had broken up and the ladies were not able to sustain the standards of golf that the members of this outstanding group had achieved. Indeed it was decided not to enter a team for the County Shield Competition in 1971, although this decision was rescinded a year later. The team struggled to compete and, in 1984, it was decided to drop out again and to substitute a series of 'friendly' matches. Another manifestation of the end of the golden era can be seen in the

85. Liverpool Society of Lady Golf Captains - Hodson Trophy 1975. From the left: Society Captain, West Lancashire Captain, Anne Bateson, Shirley Kidger (Lady Captain), Sadie Smith and Marjorie Wren.

winning scores in the Scratch Trophy, one of the trio of Barron, Reece and Shand was a winner in every year between 1950 and 1970, and the score had only once been as high as 81. During the following decade this score was only bettered twice, and on one of these occasions the winner was Alison Reece. Jennifer Marsh won the prize in three successive years from 1971, including a score of 76, and also won the Lady Derby Challenge Cup. Dilys Rimmer, Lady Captain in 1987, won the Scratch Trophy in nine out of the ten years after 1979, and since then ten new names have appeared on the board, with Dorothy Ravey, Lady Captain in 1995, being successful on four occasions. She has also made her mark in the Match Play Championship and other Club events. In 1980 Alison McLellan was the first winner of the Lancashire County's commemorative Frances Smith Trophy, which was played at Royal Birkdale. Her score included an ace at the 7th hole.

It was in 1989 that the name of a distinguished English international appeared on the S&A Honours Boards. Lora Fairclough, a member of the inland Chorley club, sought to develop her game on a dry links course, particularly during the winter months. After being extended courtesy at S&A in 1988, she joined the Club and won the Marjorie Wren Trophy and also the Scratch Trophy, with a score of 74. This was the lowest winning total since Marjorie Barron's 70, achieved over twenty years earlier. In 1991 Lora turned professional, representing Europe in the Solheim Cup in 1994, and later joining the LPGA Tour in America.

In 1992 Dian Albert set a spectacular record in a medal round, when a gross score of 90, including an air shot, gave her a nett score of 59; whilst possibly the most 'striking' achievement of recent times has been Jill Morris's score of two on Gumbley's in 1991. This was achieved with a driver and a five iron. Such successes that the lady members of the Club enjoyed in the wider world of golf, during this era, came principally in handicap events. In 1996, the County's Handicap Shield, which had eluded S&A for so long, was eventually won at Nelson, where the powerful Royal Lytham team was defeated in the final (Fig.86). The S&A team and its supporters saluted the victory with champagne; Claudette Storer had a double cause for celebration having achieved a hole in one on the 2nd hole. Jean Ball won the Bronze Meeting of the Lancashire Veteran Ladies' Golf Association in 2000.

What of the juniors? As with most clubs, efforts to promote girls' golf at S&A met with only limited success. A bright star burst briefly onto the S&A scene in 1970. Carleen Eckersley, an outstandingly talented sixteen-year-old, joined the Club, when she already had a handicap of four, held numerous

86. Lancashire Ladies' Handicap Shield 1996.
Back row from the left: Elaine Jones, Delice Fletcher, Kirsten Forbes, Dilys Rimmer, Claudette Storer,
Linda Nolte (team captain), Nancy Jenkins (Lady Captain) and Lindsay Robinson.

titles and was a member of the England Girls' and Lancashire senior team. Although still a junior, she was immediately extended the privileges of young lady status, which afforded her the opportunity to play in competitions and she won the Silver Division of the January Medal in 1971. In the same year she successfully paired with immediate past lady captain Jennifer Marsh to play in the Northern Foursomes, she also won the English Girls' Championship, and the third of her four successive Lancashire Junior Championship titles. Although she continued to be an S&A member until March 1973, all her success in representative golf, at this time, was achieved under the banner of the Hillside Club, where her parents were the caterers.

Carleen was never really a part of the junior set up at S&A, where recruitment was normally restricted to the families of members and it was a struggle to attract and to retain girls as members. Mrs. Basford, the Lady Captain in 1955, set up a committee to address this problem and a group of about ten girls was recruited. One of them recalls that they didn't play eighteen hole events. There was a series of nine hole competitions with a prize awarded for each and for an aggregate. The girls normally started at the 7th tee and they shared with the boys in the free Saturday morning golf instruction from the professional.(See Fig.78) By 1971 Dorothy Ritchie was acting as junior organiser, when there were eight girls participating. They all had handicaps; and medals and an eclectic competition were arranged during school holidays. The more successful girls were able to play in Club medals. Attention to the social side of the game came in the form of 'Girls' Teas'. Helen Bateson, one of the older girls, was particularly successful and was rewarded with ELGA coaching. Another girl, now Kathleen Whitfield, is still a Club member. The total number of girls involved seldom reached five. In 1982 the group included Debbie Mayer, the Lancashire Schools' Champion. She went on to win the Club's Silver Jubilee Trophy, the Captain's Prize and the Scratch Trophy in 1984, and the Marjorie Wren Trophy in the following year. In the process of achieving this, she reduced her handicap to five. In 1988 Victoria Davies, a sixteen-year-old, was allowed to play in the ladies' Silver Division. A former junior, Tara Marsden, won the Scratch Trophy in 1991. She succeeded in reducing her handicap from thirty-six to nine, but it was marriage, motherhood and emigration to Northern Ireland that terminated her promising S&A career. Sue McLachlan took over the mantle of junior organiser.

In addition to golfing excellence, of the kind that Marjorie Barron had demonstrated, the S&A Board also recognised other outstanding contributions made to the Club by several lady members and invited them to become honorary life associate members. Annie Sherrington, who had simultaneously held the posts of honorary secretary and honorary treasurer of the ladies' section for some thirty years from 1940, was accorded the status in 1968. Others who had contributed much to the running of the section were to follow. Judy Bunting was so honoured two years later, Marjorie Wren followed in 1974, and Dorothy Ritchie in 2003.

Judging from the number of nonagenarians in the ladies' section, active membership appears to have been something of an elixir. Marjorie Wren, the 1929 Lady Captain, had a ninetieth birthday party in 1986. Her presents from the ladies included a bottle of her favourite tipple – whisky. She was to continue to enjoy the social life of the Club into her late nineties. Her friend Dorothy Ritchie was also an active member in her nineties. Ena Sutton, who celebrated her ninetieth birthday with a dinner in 1997, was a former silver division player in the handicap team who could still be seen on the putting green and working on her swing on the practice ground in her nineties.

The minutes of the ladies' committee reveal something of the tensions that existed within the section. In most institutions the natural 'conservatism' of the establishment never sits easily with aspirations for change exhibited by younger and newer members. Coming to terms with changes in fashion such as slacks and trouser suits posed problems. When tradition dictated the eating of genteel sandwiches, toast or cakes in the ladies' lounge, toasted sandwiches presented a challenge. Although accommodation was made to allow 'business ladies' to play their competition rounds on Sundays, the efforts of this group to have annual general meetings held in the evening, or to substitute an evening dinner for the Lady Captain's tea, to enable them to participate, met stern opposition.

Bridge, along with whist and the fleetingly fashionable canasta, has been played without ever becoming a severely competitive activity, although generations of S&A members were taught to play Acoll bridge by Olive Murphy. A degree of formal structure was introduced in 1963, when a team was formed and matches arranged. Following the loss of the ladies' lounge in 2004, part of the former dining room was utilised as a card room.

After the completion of the verandah mixed lounge in 1959, the Board was slow to supply a solution to the problem of ladies having access to the bar, which was in the men's lounge. For many years they had to ring a bell and wait for service to arrive. A brief experiment to improve this service was not continued after the bar takings only amounted to eight pounds on a Thursday afternoon. As late as 1992, a gentleman member complained of his '…inability to have a drink with his wife in the same room.'

Business ladies playing their 'alternate' competition rounds on Sundays experienced difficulties booking times, as the starting sheet was only made available to them four days after the men had been able to sign up. The ladies staged a memorable day in 1996 to celebrate a hundred years of ladies' golf in Lancashire. They turned out to play wearing period dress. Inclement weather was not allowed to dampen the spirits. One placard, carried by past captain Dian Albert, highlighted the problem of tee times (Fig.87). The ladies were consistently concerned about the number of active golfers in their allowed quota of 100 members, and in 1980 they unsuccessfully approached the Board asking for an increased total, as sixty of their present members were virtually non-players. Eventually the Board allowed the number to be increased up to 110 and the overall total is currently about 120 (Fig.88).

87. Past lady captain Dian Albert's poster makes a plea first heard at S&A in 1906.

The playing membership included a number of rather inexperienced golfers and there was some reluctance on the part of novice players with the 36P handicaps to play in competitions. They were nervous about being drawn to play with more accomplished golfers. In an attempt to build their confidence, seminars on etiquette and course management were provided and special competitions played. A number improved their handicaps and were successfully encouraged to play in the normal competitions.

The Club had run an occasional amateur Ladies' Open competition before the war. It was re-introduced in 1956, but was soon dropped. A further successful revival came in 1985, when it was organised by Dorothy Graham and Dilys Rimmer. A ladies' open event now forms part of the festival.

Ladies' professional golf had made considerable strides since the war and in 1976 a Ladies' British Open Championship was launched at Fulford. S&A hosted this event three years later. The international field included a number of top amateur players, and Alison Sheard of South Africa was the champion with a score of 301 and received her prize from the Captain, Vernon Cubbon (Fig.89). Peter Alliss, the chairman of the LPGA, was a guest at this event. The ladies played from the men's yellow tees and the majority of them complained about the length of the course, although one competitor reached Gumbley's green with a drive and a seven iron. This event, which was sponsored by Pretty Polly Ltd. (stocking manufacturers), has been known as the Weetabix Women's British Open since 1987. A further Ladies' Professional Championship, sponsored by the United Friendly Insurance Society, was played at S&A in 1984. Ladies' professional golf had come a long way from the time that the solitary lady competitor played at S&A in the qualifying rounds for the Dunlop-Southport Championship in the late 1930s.

88. A strong turn out for Lady Captain Linda Nolte's Day 2005.

The relationship between the ladies' section and the men appears to have been more harmonious during the last quarter of the twentieth century. Nevertheless, changes in society's attitudes and in legislation have meant that golf clubs have had to face up to the issue of sexual equality, and S&A, like other clubs, has had to adjust to the new era. After the adoption of an equity policy in 2002 much of the administration of the ladies' sections, which had previously been done on a voluntary basis, was transferred to the professional oversight of the club secretariat. The posts of honorary secretary and honorary treasurer of the ladies' section were abolished. Separate ladies' committees were retained to run the Ladies' Open, supervise team fixtures, and look after the playing of bridge.

The 2004 clubhouse changes involved the absorption of the ladies' lounge into the new dining room, the surrender of this long cherished facility was a physical reflection of the changes that had taken place. Buildings can be changed and constitutions amended, but what of attitudes? The quotation of the view of Severiano Ballesteros, which forms the header for this chapter, is an extreme expression of the prejudice that has long dogged ladies' golf. Legislation has prompted an institutional acceptance of the principle of equality, but winning some individual hearts and minds may be a slower process.

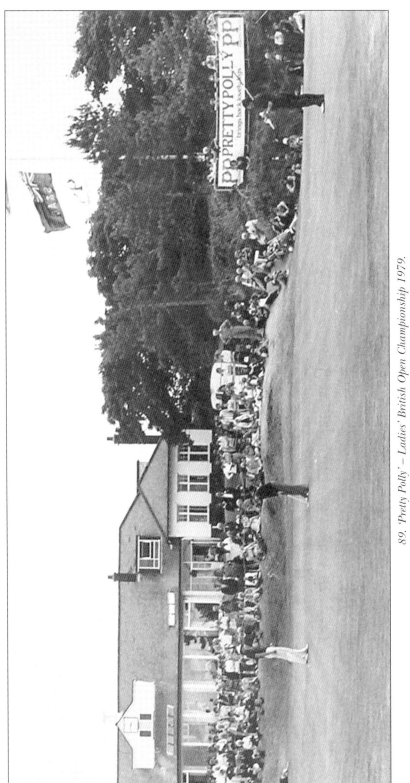

89. 'Pretty Polly' – Ladies' British Open Championship 1979.

Chapter Seven

CHAMPIONS AND CHAMPIONSHIPS

All these were honoured in their generation, and were the glory of their times.
Ecclesiasticus

As with the ladies, the post-war period also proved to be a golden age of competitive golf for the S&A men, when the membership included a trio of distinguished English internationals who between them won three English Amateur Championships.

Born into golf, Geoffrey Roberts was the youngest of the three sons of Percy Roberts, the S&A professional. The family lived near to the course, in Liverpool Avenue, and he attended the small Sacred Heart School in Liverpool Road. From there he went on to King George Vth Grammar School. Few of his contemporaries would have experienced the introduction to golf, which young Roberts enjoyed. He spent hours in his father's shop with the assistants Harry Kipling and Frank Jackson. Geoff also had the good fortune to see many of the finest golfers of their day playing in competitions at S&A. The Club made his father an honorary life member in 1933 and as such he was later able to propose his sons for junior membership. In 1937 fourteen-year-old Geoff, playing with a half set of clubs carried in a narrow 'stove-pipe' bag, won the Junior Members' Challenge Cup, off a handicap of twenty-four. He later claimed that although his father had helped him, he had never had a real golf lesson in his life. Geoff was naturally left-handed but, as with Tom Hiley, Percy Roberts insisted that he needed to change to right-handed if he was to make progress in golf.

From school Geoff went to Liverpool University, but after completing the first year of a modern language course he joined the army in 1941. Most of gunner Robert's military service was spent in India and Burma, and he was finally demobilised in 1947 and returned to his studies. He became a full member of the Club, but the long lay off from the golf had taken its toll and he struggled to regain his form. He had rarely touched a golf club whilst in the army. A great lover of cricket, which he played with distinction at school, he returned to this game and quickly earned a reputation as a dashing left-handed batsman for Ainsdale Cricket Club.

90. Geoff Roberts winner of the Boyd Quaich,
the International Students' Championship at St Andrews

Geoff then decided to concentrate on golf and in order to re-establish his handicap he submitted a number of cards and, although the scores were in the 80s and even 90s, he was given a handicap of three. Helped and encouraged by Dixie Rawlinson he was soon able to reassert himself within the Club. In 1948 he won the Easter knockout and was selected to play for Lancashire in the same year. Geoff first played in the English Amateur Championship in 1949, when it was held at nearby Formby. It was only in the sixth round that he was finally eliminated when he lost to Ronnie White, (Royal) Birkdale's outstanding Walker Cup player. His performance was sufficient to get him 'noticed' and he was selected to play in the home international series at Portmarnock. Sadly, this turned out to be a disappointing experience; he did not get a single game. The following year he won the Boyd Quaich, the International Students' Championship at St Andrews (Fig.90). After graduating in 1950 he took a post teaching at a small school in Arnside, a move that drastically reduced the opportunities for him to play golf. For this reason he resigned this post and returned to Southport, where he was to teach in two local private schools. As a teacher, participation in major competitions was restricted to those occurring during the school holidays.

Success in scratch events initially eluded him, but he was to win the Club Championship, the Captain's Prize, and the Easter knockout on three occasions each and the Blackburn Holden Cup twice. He was a regular member of the scratch team, which imposed itself on the County Team Championship in such commanding fashion. Geoff was also a member of the Hillside club and between 1956 and 1961 he won the Hillside Scratch Trophy four times and the Captain's Prize on two occasions.   He won his first individual County Championship in 1953 at Royal Lytham, his favourite course. On route to the final he narrowly defeated his friend and chauffeur on these occasions, Dixie Rawlinson. He was to win the title again in his last appearance in this championship, some ten years later. It was at Fairhaven in 1955, that he led the qualifiers to win the Rayner Batty trophy. He played for the Lancashire team up until 1964, winning nine of his twenty-two matches, that is foursome and singles encounters, and halving just one.

In the year following his 1949 debut in the English Amateur Championship, he didn't get past the qualifying stage, but in 1951 a late decision to compete at distant Hunstanton Golf Club, in Norfolk, was rewarded by him being the second lowest qualifier. He carried his good form into the knockout rounds and went on to win the Championship, in what was at that time the longest ever final.   The win finally came at the thirty-ninth hole when Geoff's approach putt for a birdie stopped just short of the hole, but in so doing it created a 'stymie' as his ball blocked the route of his opponent's putt to halve the hole.   As the rule then stood, he was under no obligation to remove his ball and his opponent conceded the hole and the match. It was shortly after this incident that a rule change took the stymie out of the game.

Pat Ward Thomas, the distinguished golf commentator, described the new champion as being: 'An excellent player with an orthodox stylish, powerful swing and fine temperament.'   The Club recognised his achievement in winning the English national title by making him an honorary life member, and members subscribed to buy him a gold cigarette case. (See Fig.73)   As English champion he was automatically selected for the home internationals, and being champion meant that he had to play at the top of the team. Although the games were played on his favourite Royal Lytham course he encountered tough opposition and won only one of his six matches. An international wilderness year followed, but his form for Lancashire was such that he was again selected in 1953. But, as in 1949, he was largely neglected and played in only one match, which he lost. Thus he was to describe his own performance at international level as being 'mediocre'.

Geoff had very fond memories of playing with two Open Champions, Argentinian Roberto de Vicenzo and Irishman Fred Daly. He was invited to play with de Vicenzo in an exhibition match at Heysham, whilst he partnered Daly in *The Daily Telegraph* Pro-Am tournament at Formby. He enjoyed his links with Irish golf and became a regular competitor in the

South of Ireland Championship, which was played annually at Lanirch Golf Club. After several near misses he won the event in 1959 and the Club holds his light blue champion's blazer.

Geoff continued to serve the Club, acting as competition and social secretary during the years in which Mrs. Woodcock was secretary to the Board. She was a pioneer of ladies' participation in this traditionally male role. In 1969 Geoff employed his literary skills to introduce a Club 'Newsletter', and also produced an illustrated account of the 1933 *Ryder Cup*. For several years Geoffrey suffered mild angina, and he died in his late seventies.

Although a few years older than Geoff Roberts, Dixon (Dixie) Rawlinson was very much one of his golfing contemporaries. As a boy he lived in Salford Road Ainsdale, his back garden overlooking the nine-hole course of the Blundell

91. Geoff Roberts English Amateur Champion 1951 – a practice swing at Hunstanton.

Golf Club. Living alongside a golf course exposed Dixie to the game from an early age. He later claimed that he had started playing golf, in 'an informal manner', at about the age of eleven. It seems highly likely that, as at S&A, local boys might have played on this course without permission. The Blundell Club was disbanded in 1935, when Dixie was about eighteen. Juvenile membership of S&A was still limited to the families of members at this time, but as a teenager he spent some of his time as one of the Club's part-time caddies. His son Mark tells of how the caddies and other local youngsters played golf on their own three-hole 'sand course', behind the clubhouse. Thus he had developed some golfing skills before joining the S&A Artisans' Section. Although his name does not appear on its honours

131

boards he did win a silver Artisan Golfers' Association medal, presented in association with the *News of the World*, at the eleventh annual North of England Artisans' Tournament in 1938.

After the outbreak of war Dixie enlisted in the army. He served in Palestine and then in Burma. Following his post-war discharge he returned to golf as an artisan, but by 1947 he had applied for and been accepted as a member of the parent club; he was then thirty-years old. Although he had no opportunity to play golf during the war it seems that his swing and game was already '...much the same as it was later in his greatest years.' He quickly became scratch without ever having had a lesson, but he did acknowledge that Percy Roberts had shown him how to hold the club with the Vardon grip. 'I got going by reading instructional books,' he said, 'Sam Snead was the one I followed and I tried to develop on his methods.' Geoff Roberts described Dixie as a player with '...a wide smooth swing' who gave the appearance of never having to force a shot (Fig.92). 'His iron play was good and his short game equally so.' An idiosyncratic looking wedge - 'Black Jack' - became a legendary weapon.

92. Dixie Rawlinson driving in a charity exhibition match at Withington Golf Club 1950.
From the left: A.D. Cairncross (the home professional), Henry Cotton and Ronnie White.

Although a successful international golfer, Dixie never won his national title. His best chance of success came at the Royal Cinque Ports course in 1950. Having qualified comfortably he reached the semi-final stage before suffering an unexpected, if narrow, defeat. Dixie's international debut had come a year earlier in the home internationals, played at Portmarnock. It was as a member of this team that the other S&A debutant, Geoff Roberts, failed to get a single game. Dixie's international career lasted from 1949 until 1961. He played in thirty games, winning thirteen, losing fifteen and halving two. Selection for the Walker Cup team to play against the United States of America appeared to be a possibility in 1949 and again in 1951. But, following trials in which he performed well, he was not selected for the team.

Leonard Crawley, writing in *The Daily Telegraph* described him as '…a thoroughly competent golfer with a compact and strictly modern style. When addressing the ball his hands are too low. This leads to too much rigidity and sergeant major golf.' He believed that Dixie's method was too mechanical. On another occasion he wrote that Dixie '…appeared to me to be a player who knows what he is trying to do and can generally do it.' Dixie gained the reputation of being most assiduous in practising.

Dixie is probably best remembered as a stalwart of the Lancashire county team. He played his first match in 1948 and his career ended in 1975. He played 101 times for the county, losing just over a third of these matches. It must be remembered that most of his matches were played at the top of the team. Only ten players, out of the almost 500 who have represented Lancashire, have notched up the coveted century. Having enjoyed such a distinguished playing career it is not surprising that he later became county captain. He was also a very consistent performer in the County Championship. Dixie was the leading qualifier, and thus winner of the Rayner Batty Trophy, on seven occasions. At Hillside, in 1954, he broke the course record by three, when he scored 68 in the first round. He set another record when he added a 70 for an aggregate qualifying score of 138, a score, which has since been equalled but not bettered. His record in the Rayner Batty suggests that he was a strong medal player. In fact he only failed to qualify for the knockout stage on one occasion. Despite this outstanding record at the qualifying stage, it was 1956 before he won the first of his two championships, this success was achieved on his home course (Fig.93). The *Manchester Guardian* correspondent wrote that: 'Strangely Rawlinson's accomplishments, so high in the gentle atmosphere of stroke-building, have not revealed themselves with the same power to destroy an opponent in combat; he has so often failed when the prize was seemingly so firmly in his

*93. Dixie Rawlinson receiving the Lancashire Championship Trophy
from Lord Derby at S&A in 1956. A.R. Ball the S&A Captain looks on.*

keeping.' It comes as no surprise that he should hold a number of course records. At S&A he broke the record set by Sam Robinson, he also set records at North Shore, Blackpool and at Wilpshire.

Dixie's strength at medal play was perhaps best demonstrated by his performance in the Open Championship, when it was played at Royal Lytham in 1952. He came within two shots of winning the Silver Medal for the leading amateur, and was thirty-third overall. Unfortunately he bunkered his drive on the seventy-second hole and dropped two shots. By this final round he was a tired man and his score of 80 was his highest of the championship.

Dixie was a regular competitor in open amateur events in the region, spare seats in his car always being available to fellow competitors from S&A. Geoff Roberts wrote that: 'Dixie had those two necessities for a successful amateur golfer – an understanding wife and a generous employer.' In fact Dixie worked for a corn broker and it seems that he had to use part of his holiday entitlement to compete in many events. Living in Hillside, he regularly took advantage of access to the course from the north end and played until failing light forced him to quit.

He did have other interests outside golf. Dixie was a Southport amateur ballroom champion and competed in the British Amateur Ballroom Championship. Demonstrations of the Rawlinsons' dancing skills were a feature of Club social functions.

Dixie had an inexhaustible appetite for competitive golf and played in every club competition for which he was available, including mixed foursomes with his wife Peggy. Not surprisingly he amassed a formidable record of success in the major club events. He won the Scratch Trophy on ten occasions, the Easter knockout five times, and the Captain's Prize once. A born leader, Dixie was captain of every Club team that he played in. He was a confident and humorous public speaker and he amply demonstrated this skill on the occasion of being made an honorary life member in 1973. Dixon's contributions to the Club were not restricted to the course. From 1958 he served on the Board, and was an active member of both Green and Handicap Committees.

Always a canny player, advancing years saw his nickname change to the 'Grey Fox', and later the 'Old Grey Fox'. Through the winter, about ten of his friends would join him in the corner of the lounge every Wednesday night. The conviviality in 'Scratch Corner' was legendary. A heart complaint was to make walking the course difficult for Dixie, but permission from the Board to use a buggy meant that he didn't have to retire from the game. Indeed his golf was given a new lease of life. Off a handicap of four, a nett 68 won him the Woodvale Trophy and a handicap reduction to three. His performance off this handicap gained him the David Marsh Trophy for the best nett aggregate score for the four rounds of the Spring and Autumn Meetings in 1978.

Dixie's enthusiasm for playing the game was as strong as ever, and, on a very cold Saturday in December 1978, when few members had ventured out onto the course, he persuaded three of his friends to join him for six holes. After these had been played he suggested that they should continue on the 7th and 8th and then come back down the 6th fairway. Back in the locker room Dixie collapsed, and, after emergency treatment he was taken to the hospital, where he died in the early hours of the Sunday morning.

The third member of S&A's post-war trinity of English internationals is David Marsh. Another local boy, his home was in Lynton Drive at the north end of the course. David is very proud of the fact that the house in which he was born was built on part of the 1907 course. His mother and father were both members and at the age of nine David became a junior member. Along with the other youngsters at S&A he played throughout the summer holidays. He particularly values the opportunities that were afforded to play senior/junior foursomes and the experience of playing with Tom Hiley, Dixie Rawlinson and Geoff Roberts (Fig.94). He also recalls help that he received from Sam Robinson. Sam was still an active golfer. It was 1949 before the EGU agreed to the Club 'increasing' Sam's handicap to scratch! Sam won the Captain's Prize in the following year, and he was congratulated at the AGM in 1961 for having a gross 78 in the *News of the World* Tournament qualifying competition. Sam died a few years later at the age of seventy-nine.

David rapidly reduced his handicap. Playing in the national boys' championship in 1950 earned him a place on the English Boys' Team in the following year. On leaving King George Vth School, he went up to Cambridge University and was awarded a golfing blue. He followed Geoff Roberts's example and won the Boyd Quaich at St Andrews in 1957, with a record score of 66 in the first round. Not surprisingly the Old Course, which was to figure so significantly in his later career, was to become his favourite course. His medical training was completed at Liverpool University, and he qualified in 1959.

94. David Marsh and Dixie Rawlinson on the 1st tee during a match against Cambridge University 1956.

In the early 1960s golf took second place to professional and family life, but after a gap of some four years he did return to serious play. He was persuaded by Michael Bonallack and Michael Lunt to enter the English Amateur Championship in 1964. He agreed and his caddie was Dr. George Foster, the brother of Rodney Foster, whom he was to defeat in the thirty-six-hole final, after having been four holes in arrears. To celebrate this success, he was made an honorary life member of the Club and received a silver salver from the members, and a fountain pen from the ladies' section. In 1967 he was the youngest ever S&A captain, at the age of thirty-three. Three years later the English Championship was played at Royal Birkdale. David reached the final and, after being four holes down, he again came back, this time to win by 6 and 4. The correspondent from *Golf Illustrated* wrote:

> There can hardly have been a more popular success...His delightful personality, linked with his considerable ability and his stout heart, have made him one of the best liked and respected amateur players of the game.

Many S&A members were able to support David on this occasion. To mark his success the David Marsh Trophy, a fine sculpted figure of a marsh harrier, was introduced for an S&A open senior event.

Between 1956 and 1972 David played seventy-five games for England losing only twenty-eight of them. He was the captain of the team between 1968 and 1971. Probably the best remembered incident of David's playing career came in the Walker Cup. It is given to few amateur golfers to make a public impression of the magnitude that he achieved. He was first selected for the Walker Cup squad for the 1959 match at Muirfield, a time when he was involved in his medical examinations. Golf had been neglected and he felt that he was in such poor form that he informed the selectors that he should not be chosen to play in any match. Nevertheless he was included in the team to play at St Andrews in 1971. It was this team that broke the stranglehold that the United States had exercised on the trophy since 1938, and it was David whom history placed at the centre of this achievement. His game against Bill Hyndman III, a golfer of considerable pedigree, was the only one left on the course. The overall score stood with the United States having won eleven games and the Great Britain and Ireland team twelve. A win for the United States would be sufficient for them tie the match and thus to retain the trophy as the current holders. The pair arrived at the 17th tee with the match level. Playing the infamous 'Road Hole', at this critical juncture, David hit a majestic three iron second shot into the heart of this difficult green to set up a win. He later modestly told a reporter that he had

95. David Marsh playing an iron shot c.1971.

'...hit the 17th green for the first time in the series.' This shot was described in Peter Alliss's *Illustrated History of Golf* as '...one of the finest strokes of the decade, given the circumstances.' A half in four on the 18th gave the game to David and the Walker Cup to the home team (Fig.95).

Surprisingly he was never Lancashire Champion, although he twice led the qualifiers to take the Rayner Batty Trophy. He did play in forty-eight matches for the Lancashire team, winning twenty-three and losing only sixteen.

After a period at Sefton Hospital he joined a practice in Kirkby and then played much of his club golf at nearby Ormskirk. Nevertheless, he did manage to achieve a formidable record in competitions at S&A. He won the Scratch Trophy on five occasions between 1967 and 1979; he was successful in the Easter Competition in 1952; and carried off the Captain's Prize three times, between 1951 and 1959.

David became a major figure in the administration of the game. He was non-playing captain of the Walker Cup team in 1973 and 1975, as well as a selector for eight years, four of them as chairman. A member of the Royal and Ancient Golf Club, he became a member, then chairman, of its Rules of Golf Committee, and was Captain of this, the most prestigious golf club in the world, in 1990 (Fig.96). He had also been President of the English Golf Union in 1988, and served as a junior selector. At the regional level he had

96. St Andrews 1990. David Marsh driving-in as Captain of the R&A.

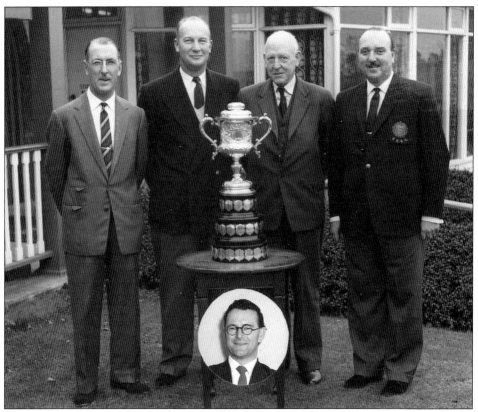

97. Lancashire Club Champions at Royal Lytham 1960.
From the left: Dixie Rawlinson, Tom Hiley, J. Bonar Wood (Captain), Jackie Wroe, inset Geoff Roberts.

been President of the Lancashire Union of Golf Clubs in 1985. Such is David's record that it came as no surprise when, in 1998, he received the Gerald Micklem Award for his outstanding contribution to amateur golf. At S&A, he also served as Chairman of the Board.

Tom Hiley's blossoming representative golf career had been crucially interrupted by the outbreak of war and service in the Far East with the Royal Air Force. Post war demands of business - Ainsdale Laundry - appeared to make it difficult for him to give time to the game. In the early years after his return from India, the time that he spent in the rough led his friends to nickname him 'Jungle Boy'. No longer the tall slim figure of his youth, Geoff Roberts believed that he was never able '...to capture again his wonderful fluid swing with its great wide shoulder turn', or match the level of excellence that he had previously attained. In order to gain consistency from the tee, he shortened his back swing and despite sacrificing some length, such was his talent, that he was able to enjoy considerable success at club and county levels. Although the excellence of his golf might have diminished, it appears that he came near to gaining full international honours. Both Geoff Roberts and Dixie Rawlinson were selected for the home internationals in 1949. At least one golf journalist speculated that if a surgical operation had not intervened, Tom might have raised the Club's representation in this event to three. He played for the county team up until 1960 winning twenty-one of his forty-one games; he also won the Rayner Batty Trophy in the 1956 championship. In Club events he won the Captain's Prize on a further three occasions, and the Scratch Prize six times. His last major success was his third win of the Sam Robinson Trophy in 1973. He was regarded as the perfect foursome partner, with his ability to lay the ball dead from around the green and to sink those troublesome short putts time and again. In his later years he served on the Club Board and was chairman of the Green Committee. In addition to the individual County Championship, there was a competition for a club team of four with the lowest aggregate score. The S&A team was to dominate this event. After the Championship was revived in 1948, S&A was the champion club in fourteen out of the next sixteen years. This included a run of eleven consecutive wins. Furthermore in two of these years S&A second team were the runners-up. Robert Browning, the prolific golf writer, judged that: 'Apart from one or two specially circumstanced clubs…there are few in the country who can match S&A for the number of top class players in its ranks.' Geoff Roberts names Tom Hiley, Dixie Rawlinson, Jim Telfer-Shiel, Jackie Wroe, and Bruce Naylor as the stalwarts of the squad (Fig.97). Jackie Wroe, a local boy who had been a caddie at S&A and one of the pre-war group who played on the 'sand course', was a Northumberland county player who joined S&A from Hillside in 1950. Jackie was the Lancashire Champion in 1951, when he beat Dixie Rawlinson in the final. He played forty-three games for Lancashire and was later the county senior champion. When the Open Championship was played at Royal Birkdale in 1954, Jackie qualified to play in all four rounds. In 1949 S&A had eighteen members with handicaps of four or less. Leonard Crawley, *The Daily Telegraph* columnist, reported that the Club could field a first team of eight with a handicap average nearer to plus one than to scratch. Geoff Roberts claimed that it was 'The success of this squad that gave rise to the legend of S&A as a nursery for producing outstanding amateur talent.' Michael Reece was another fine player who came through the junior ranks at S&A, although much of his representative golf was played under the aegis of his later membership of the Formby Club. (See Fig.105) In addition to the home grown talent, leading players from other Lancashire clubs chose to also become members at Ainsdale and play some of their golf on a seaside links course, in a highly competitive environment. Two Lancashire Champions – Jackie Jones from Grange Park and Dave Anderson

141

*98. Stephenson Winter League Champions 1968-69. S&A captain Bill Wilding receiving the cup from the Captain of Ormskirk Golf Club. From the right: Mark Rawlinson, David Marsh, Dixie Rawlinson, Tom Hiley, Joe Moore (Sports' Editor **Southport Visiter**), Brian Williams.*

from Leigh –were amongst their number, along with Welsh International Ivor Thomas from Formby. Lew Seagar, a county player from West Derby, played in two of S&A's Lancashire Championship winning teams. It was Jackie Jones who pipped Dixie Rawlinson for the Silver Medal in the Open Championship at Royal Lytham in 1952. Dominance on the scale achieved in the early post-war years was not maintained, but the Club remained the most successful in Lancashire, through to the end of the millennium. The twenty-five county championship successes achieved by S&A dwarf the five wins of Hillside, the closest challenger. In 1969, there were sixteen Category One golfers (handicaps scratch to three) playing regularly at the Club. It was believed that this was possibly the largest number in the country.

Apart from the County Championship, which was completed in one weekend, low handicap golfers had limited opportunity to represent their club in team events. There was a demand for such fare and in 1968 a new competition was brought into being. This Stephenson Newspapers' Winter League became the *Southport Visiter* Winter Scratch League and later came under the auspices of a newly formed Southport and District Golf Association (Fig.98). Seven local clubs, including S&A, initially participated, and two others joined later. The Association's first Chairman was S&A's Michael Edwards. Although the zenith of the Club's golfing excellence had passed, it remained a considerable force and soon established a strong record in the Association's events. The Winter League was won in nine out of its first fifteen seasons. The 1980s were fallow years, but four more wins came in the 1990s and a further win in 2003-4. Successes also came in the Team Tournament and the Summer Matchplay Competition, when the Association's programme was expanded. The *Lancashire Evening Post* also organised a scratch competition, which S&A dominated throughout its relatively short life. After winning the trophy five times in six years it was awarded to S&A outright (Fig.99). In 1974 Churchmans sponsored a national club championship. S&A qualified for this 'Grandee Cigar' competition as winners of the Lancashire Championship but lost in the final at Sunningdale to Moor Park.

99. Winners of the Lancashire Evening Post Trophy 1987.
From the left: Nick Lucas, Paul Bagshaw, Paul Gwynne, Jim O'Rourke (Captain),
*a representative of the **Lancashire Evening Post**, Tony Jackson, Frank Till and Mike Edwards.*

A further opportunity for competitive scratch team golf came when the Club was invited to enter a team in an invitation event – an inter-club scratch foursomes competition mounted by the Royal Liverpool Club, to mark its centenary in 1969. The Captain, the former speaker of the House of Commons, the Rt. Hon. Selwyn Lloyd, M.P., presented a trophy and the annual competition became known as the Selwyn Lloyd Bowl. This trophy was won in 1970, 1974, 1975, 1978, 1984 and 1999. S&A had previously re-instituted annual scratch team matches with Royal Liverpool. Annual scratch team matches were also played with Hesketh, for the Ainsketh Trophy, and

100. Irish Inter-Provincial Championship at Royal Dublin 1956. Mike Edwards (left) with Walker Cup star Joe Carr and his son Jodi.

Fairhaven, for the Fairdale Salver. The Club's reputation in competitive golf led to requests for matches from a wide variety of sources. Games were played with teams from London, Cambridge and Oxford universities. The Bolton and District Golf Association provided regular quality opposition. A team, including the professional, annually contested the West Lancashire Club's Crosby Beacon, winning on four occasions.

Major golfing figures in more recent years have included Michael Edwards, an Irish international player between 1956 and 1962, who joined the Club in 1968 (Fig.100). He rapidly became a stalwart of the scratch team and played for Lancashire between 1970 and 1975 losing only two of his nineteen games. Nevertheless, such was the competition for places in the Club's scratch teams in this era, that in his first season he had to be content with playing in the second string. Stephen Rooke, a local youngster, who reached the quarter-final of the English Amateur Championship, when it was won by

David Marsh in 1970, and was a runner-up for the prestigious Brabazon Trophy, played seventeen matches for Lancashire; whilst Brian and John Williams also played in this decade. More recently Paul Bagshaw, Raife Hutt, Philip Bird and Mark Bailey were also selected. In all, seventeen S&A members have represented Lancashire since the Second World War. In addition, Martin Wild, an Ashton-on-Mersey member who also joined S&A, played for Lancashire in 100 games between 1978 and 1994. He won the County Championship in 1981 and 1986, and was runner-up in 1993; whilst Michael Reece played for Lancashire seventy-eight times and won the Championship in 1971 and 1976.

Raife Hutt was a player of the modern era, who, in a brief amateur career, scaled the heights achieved by earlier S&A golfing giants (Fig.101). He was a full international between 1991 and 1993, playing in twenty-three games for England, losing only eight of them. Hutt also won the Lancashire Championship in 1992, and followed it by being runner-up in the English Amateur Championship in the same year. He set an amateur course record at S&A with a score of 64.

Within the Club, competition was always keen. In 1984 the average winning score in all stroke play competitions was five under the standard scratch score. Michael Edwards dominated scratch events in the 1970s and early 1980s, winning thirteen trophies during this period. He and his wife Hilary also shared an outstanding record of success in the Club's mixed foursomes competition. They won the trophy, which they had donated, in six consecutive years. Exceptionally, Paul Bagshaw managed to win the Easter Meeting, Scratch Trophy, Scratch Match Play, David Marsh Trophy and the Dixon Rawlinson Trophy in 1987 (Fig.102). His collection of scratch trophies is now approaching twenty. Around the end of the millennium, the name of Alan Harrison became prominent on the honours' boards, some ten years after he won the Easter Meeting as a junior member. He followed Brian Williams as the scratch team captain and was also an industrious worker on Club committees (Fig.103). In 2001 he won five of the Club's major trophies, set a new course record of 68, and shared a victory in the Family Foursomes with his son Jonathan. An unusual achievement was the scoring of nine consecutive twos on par three holes. Alan was to achieve national prominence in 2005 when, after two rounds of the English Open Men's Mid-Amateur Championship for the Logan Trophy, he shared the lead three strokes clear of the field. Sadly he surrendered this lead on the final hole and was beaten by a single shot to finish in third place.

101. Raife Hutt enjoyed a short but distinguished career as an amateur.
102. Paul Bagshaw 1987 – a vintage year.
103. Scratch Team 2002. Back row from the left: Simon Aplin, Phil Bird, Alan Harrison,
Gary Gillespie, Ian Leadbetter, Joel Rodwell, Geoff Fallows, Chris Walker (Captain),
Paul Bagshaw, Mike O'Brien.

The success of the scratch teams probably contributed to the emergence of S&A as a prolific nursery for young would-be golfers. Although junior membership had been opened up to none family members, the sons of distinguished golfing members figured prominently in the ranks of S&A juniors (Fig.104). Mark Rawlinson won the Southport and District Boys' Challenge Cup in 1963 and gained English junior international honours in 1967. Paul Bagshaw, Robert Sturgeon, and Martin Till played for the county boys' team in 1981. In the following year David Aspinall was the Lancashire Schoolboy Champion. Anthony Jackson played for the county team for three years from 1985 and in 1987 he won the Lancashire Boys' Championship, a title won by his club mate Raife Hutt in the following year. Hutt also captained the Lancashire Boys' Team, and later played for the British and Irish youth team. He was the runner-up in the British Youth Championship when Jim Payne, the current S&A professional, won this event. Jonathan Large and Steve Younger were both winners in their own age group of the Lancashire Boys' Championship of 1987. Jonathan was later selected for the English Schools' Team in 1990 and 1991. In 1992 Tony Meekin played for the Lancashire Boys' Team. The Southport and District Golf Association introduced a competition for under eighteen-year-olds in 1990. The S&A youngsters have won this Summer League on three occasions, an achievement only bettered by Hillside with four victories. Ian Leadbetter was the individual under eighteen champion in 2004.

104. Bootle Junior Golf Championship 1961. Four S&A members from the left:
Simon Bunting (11 years), Paul Hiley (11), P. Kirkman (13) and Mark Rawlinson (11).

A Liverpool and District Colts' Challenge Cup had been contested since the early 1930s, and S&A decided to enter a team in 1938. The competition lapsed during the war and was only revived in 1958, and S&A's team was to win the cup in the following three years (Fig.105). The successful 1966 team included Paul Hiley, Mark Rawlinson, Colin Davies and Michael Pearson, who all played for Lancashire Colts (Fig.106). The Challenge Cup was again won in 1973 and 1976. Brian Williams was selected for Lancashire Colts in 1976 and Frank Till in 1977. The colts enjoyed fuller playing rights than the juniors, but the Club allowed a few outstanding young junior golfers, such as Michael Reece, to be fast tracked into the colts from the age of sixteen. This decision helped to promote the golfing development of a number of boys. Former S&A juniors, Paul Bagshaw, Anthony Jackson and Raife Hutt all went on to play for Lancashire Colts, as did Steve Ainscough.

The apparent decline in the recent level of achievement on the part of the S&A's youngsters is probably a function of other clubs catching up on their youth programmes. Nevertheless, the S&A conveyor belt continues to deliver talented young players. Joel Rodwell won the Scratch Prize in 2003 and 2004 and the Dixon Rawlinson Trophy in 2003. All the Club trophies continue to be enthusiastically contested and the competition to share the honours boards with S&A's golfing greats remains as keen as ever (Fig.107).

105. Colts' Team 1958. Back row from the left: Tom Chatterton, John Graham, Michael Reece, John Yates, Norman Parry, David Marsh, Fred Brewer (Captain), and John Eccles.

106. Colts' Team 1966. Back row from the left: Paul Hiley, Mark Rawlinson, Jerry Barber, Colin Davies, John Williams, Ian Rogerson, C.B. Smith (Captain), Tony Buckels, and Derek Hicks.

107. Presentation of the Captain's Prize 2005 by Errol Cheesman to Gary Cooper. Paul Shawcross was the runner-up.

Chapter Eight

THE PROFESSIONALS: A NEW ERA

Gary Wolstehholme said 'You stand on this course (Ganton, the venue of the 2003 Walker Cup) and think, God has put his hand on this place', whereas at a home Ryder Cup you'd be more likely to hear someone say 'You stand on this course and think, God, someone's forked out a few quid to bring it here.' The last pure golfing venue for the Ryder Cup was Walton Heath in 1981. Since then the size of the chequebook has counted for more than the quality of the terrain.

Martin Johnson **The Daily Telegraph** 2003

After the war, professional golf tournaments returned to S&A; the Southport Corporation favoured a re-start of the Dunlop-Southport Tournament in 1945, but the Dunlop Company said it preferred to wait a further year. The total prize money was £2,000 and the financial liability of the Corporation was limited to £1,500. The Corporation ran the tournament with the General Manager of the Publicity and Attractions Department acting as secretary and the Borough Treasurer as treasurer. The final stages of the 1946 tournament were played at S&A, the eventual winner being Max Faulkner, the colourful self-styled clown prince of golf who was later to become Open Champion (Fig.108).

After the 1946 tournament, which had cost it £1,480, the Corporation decided to pull out as the joint sponsor. Following representations from the Company, Southport agreed to be involved again in 1948. The final stages returned to S&A and the Ulsterman Fred Daly, who won the Open in the same year, took the title. The tournament itself was still the long drawn out affair that had caused Cotton to boycott it. There were two qualifying rounds followed by four rounds in the competition proper and if, as was the case in 1948, there was a tie, a further thirty-six holes were played. Such were the escalating costs of this competition that the Corporation had to find £3,000 as its fifty per cent contribution. It proved to be too expensive and the tournament was dropped. There were still insufficient tournaments to allow professionals to rely on them for their income. Consequently the competitions usually finished on a Friday in order to allow the professionals to return to their shops for the weekend.

108. Dunlop-Southport Tournament 1948.
Max Faulkner, who had won this event in 1946, driving on the 5th tee.

A relatively cheap form of professional golf to mount was an exhibition match involving only four players, often including two local amateurs. The Publicity and Attractions Committee received a request to play such a match in Southport in 1946. It too was played at S&A, when two teams contested a £500 'Empire Challenge Match' over thirty-six holes (Fig.109). Dai Rees of Wales, the star of the 1937 Ryder Cup team who played in a further eight such matches and was captain on four occasions, and Charlie Ward of England played against Norman Von Nida, the diminutive Australian with his distinctive back beret, and Bobby Locke, a South African who won the Open on three occasions, and who invariably played wearing plus fours and a flat cap. Despite atrocious weather conditions, with heavy rain driven by gale force winds, S&A again delivered the gallery and approximately 2,000 spectators followed the match.

109. Empire Challenge Match 1946.
From the left: Dai Rees, Norman von Nida, Charlie Ward, Bobby Locke and the Mayor of Southport.

There was still some professional golf played at S&A in the late 1940s and 1950s. The Club's scratch team played an annual one-day match against a team of professionals representing the Liverpool Alliance, playing foursomes in the morning and singles in the afternoon (Fig.110). The match was the brainchild of Crewe Roden, the honorary secretary of S&A, and Bert Standish, who was captain in 1961 and was also President of the Alliance. John Burton, the Hillside professional, selected the professional teams. They included Eric Green of Huyton and Prescot, Ted Jarman of West Lancashire, and Bill Davies of Wallasey, all Ryder Cup players. Initially the professionals gave the amateurs a three-hole start in each match, but experience rapidly dictated that this should be reduced to two holes. Retired Dean Wood professional Tony Coop still complains at having been required to give such a lead to David Marsh. Playing in these matches was deemed to have sharpened the competitive edge of the scratch team members. It may be just a coincidence that it was after these matches started in 1948 that the Club should enjoy its extraordinary run of success in the Lancashire County Team Championship. In 1969 the fixture's twenty-first anniversary was celebrated and the S&A team included Tom Hiley and Geoff Roberts, who had played in the inaugural match. After years of closely

110. Match with Merseyside professionals 1957.
Back row, from the left: Harry Rudd (West Derby), Guy Taylor (Sec. Merseyside Alliance), Jimmy Large, Geoff Roberts,
Bill Almond, Charlie Blackshaw, Harry Large sen. (Childwall), Ken Davies, Norman Saul, Jackie Wroe,
Centre row: Jack McLachlan (S&A), Eric Green (Huyton and Prescot), John Burton (Hillside),
Stuart Cullen (Captain), Dixie Rawlinson, Vic Harries (Leasowe), Reg Hallam (Woolton),
Front row: Tony Coop (Dean Wood), David Marsh, Mike Reece, Bob Jarman (Prenton), and Vic Howard.

contested matches followed by splendid social occasions, the professionals sought to restrict the event to an afternoon only. There were also whisperings about them wanting some form of financial reward for taking part. Whatever the truth the series ended soon afterwards.

In 1953 Dunlop attempted unsuccessfully to revive its arrangement with Southport to mount an annual professional tournament. It was proposed to increase the prize fund to £2,200 and the Company was prepared to pay the Corporation for all the expenses incurred in running the tournament. The Dunlop Two Thousand Guineas Golf Tournament was played at S&A in 1954 (Fig.111). South African Bobby Locke was the winner but severe gales completely destroyed the catering marquee and the following year the event was replaced by the Swallow Penfold Tournament. The Irish Ryder Cup player, Christie O'Connor senior, won this event, which was not repeated.

S&A was involved in an early venture into establishing competitive golf for older professionals. In 1954 the Club hosted an unofficial world veteran championship. This thirty-six-hole event, again part sponsored by the

Southport Corporation, brought together the nostalgic pairing of fifty-one-year-old Percy Alliss and former Open Champion Gene Sarazen, who was fifty-seven. It was, of course, a reprise of an earlier Ryder Cup tussle at S&A (Fig.112). Sarazen was in Southport primarily to play in the Open Championship at Royal Birkdale. Thus the match with Alliss clashed with the popular practice days for the Open. In addition weather conditions were poor, and in the event very few paying spectators were attracted to S&A.

111. The Dunlop 2,000 Guineas Tournament 1954.

1959 saw the playing of an unusual but popular event at S&A. It was a two-day match between a team of amateurs and a team of professionals. It was billed as a practice match for the Walker and Ryder Cup teams and attracted much national publicity. The professionals won a closely contested match, in which S&A's David Marsh overwhelmed his professional opponent, R.P. Mills from Pinner Hill, winning by an 8 and 7 margin.

After the demise of the Dunlop-Southport tournaments, regular professional golf was no longer a feature of S&A, but in 1962 there was an opportunity to see Jack Nicklaus playing at S&A, in what was his first professional tournament in this country. Hillside was hosting the event on behalf of Carreras, the tobacco company who were promoting a new brand of cigarettes – Piccadilly. Every competitor played one of his two qualifying rounds at S&A. Jack Nicklaus, who had enjoyed a glittering amateur career, later described his appearance in this competition as one of the dumbest things of his professional career. It seems that in these early days as a professional he '...was still not absolutely sure of his (my) earning capabilities as a pro' and 'decided that this might be an opportunity for

112. An international seniors' challenge match 1954.
Percy Alliss (right) and Gene Sarazen.

some easy pickings.' The total prize money was £8,000, with £2,000 for the winner. These were the highest figures that had been played for in Great Britain, and the highest ever outside America. Coming from temperatures in the nineties at Fort Worth, Texas, with little time for adjustment, Nicklaus found the weather was cold, wet and windy. He also experienced difficulty with the smaller ball, then in use in this country, and having to play with an unfamiliar set of irons, which he had to represent whilst he was here (Fig.113). There was no practice ground at S & A and it is claimed that before going to the first tee, Nicklaus stood on the grass patch in front of the clubhouse windows, and boomed three drives over the railway and on to what was then part of Hillside course, and is now Ainsdale Hope High School. The *Southport Visiter* noted that the '...most disappointing feature of a day of fine golf was the failure of the American golfer, Jack Nicklaus, to live up to his high reputation.' One of the few spectators who watched him play recalls him hitting a violent hook off the 14th (now 15th) tee. The event was won by the Australian Peter Thomson, a five times winner of the Open Championship. Only the top thirty competitors collected any money and Nicklaus, with a modest score of 298 for the four rounds, qualified for the last of these prizes. He did, however, go on to win the US Open in the same year and then a further seventeen major championships.

Three years later, in 1965, S&A members had the opportunity to see another American golfing great playing their course. The player was Arnold Palmer,

114. Roosevelt Memorial Polio Nine Nations Tournament 1965.
Arnold Palmer completing his round.

113. The Piccadilly Tournament 1962.
Jack Nicklaus with his caddie Bill Tomlinson, whose sons
Bill and George were both assistant professionals at S&A.

winner of the Open Championship in 1961 and 1962, the event a Roosevelt Memorial Polio Fund Nine Nations Tournament (Fig.114). This well-supported venture was held on the Sunday prior to the Open Championship being played at Royal Birkdale. The strong international field consisted of players who did not have to play in the qualifying rounds for the Open and also included Gary Player, the current American Open Champion. Sebastian Miguel of Spain, who set a course record of 71, won the tournament. Palmer took third place.

The Texaco Pro-Am was played at S&A in 1972 and 1973. Held to raise money for the National Society for Cancer Relief in the first year and the World Wildlife Fund in the second, teams of two professionals played with a celebrity amateur, in Texaco's first venture at sponsoring a tournament in this country. A prize fund of £7,500 helped to attract the professionals, whilst the celebrities were drawn mainly from the worlds of show business and sport. The inclusion of international entertainers such as Bing Crosby and Sean Connery playing with golfers of the stature of the South African Gary Player ensured that the public supported these events in numbers (Fig.115). The turnout in 1972 was estimated at 8,200. The leading professional, with a score of 66, six under par, was Ryder Cup player Peter Oosterhuis, later a distinguished TV commentator.

115. Texaco Pro-Am 1973. Gary Player, Bing Crosby and Bruce Forsyth.

Through the 1980s and 1990s members of old established clubs, such as S&A, might have found it odd that clubs which had done so much to foster the development of the PGA and the professional game, so rarely figured as hosts for professional events. The explanation is relatively simple, professional golf was organised by the European Tour and its hierarchy of associated satellite tours. They appear to have 'sold' their events to the highest bidder and were invariably played on proprietary courses seeking to publicise these venues through the extensive media coverage that the game attracted. It seems that support for the professional game, which was so freely provided by clubs in the past, counted for nothing in this hard-headed commercial world. When the PGA celebrated its centenary in 2001 it did mark the contributions made by clubs in past years. S&A was one of those to receive a certificate of thanks. A gift of a commemorative oak, grown from an acorn from the Oakland Hills course in America, was planted on the course. The curious can now find this unmarked tree on the grass patch behind the car park.

These changes in the promotion of the professional game meant the leading professionals seldom played at club courses such as S&A. Members had to be satisfied with such special occasions as the visit of five-times Open Champion Tom Watson, coming to the Club to give a public golfing clinic in 1991 on behalf of the company whose equipment he then used.

There is still one major professional event that remains in 'amateur' hands. The event is the 'Open Championship', and the safe hands are those of the Royal and Ancient Golf Club of St Andrews. The Open is always contested on one of Great Britain's great links courses. Such is its appeal to competitors that a qualifying procedure has to be employed. Formerly, after regional pre-qualifying rounds had been played, there was still a need to play thirty-six hole qualifying events on a number of courses in the vicinity of the links at which the Open was being played. These were played over the weekend prior to the Open. S&A has regularly been invited to act as one of these courses, when the Open has been played on this coast. The R&A paid clubs for participating, and members and general public had the opportunity to see, at no charge, outstanding emerging and declining golfers, particularly from overseas, playing on their courses. One of the great delights was being able to walk with the players along the fairways and follow the fortunes of an individual group around the course, thus seeing rounds being built and shots being played, from close up. This is a pleasure no longer available at the great golfing events because of the huge crowds they attract. Orville Moody, a US Open Champion and idiosyncratic cross-hand putter, played at S&A in 1969. A qualifier in 1976 was Doug Sanders, the American who had so dramatically failed to hole a short putt on the 18th green at St Andrews to win the Open a few years earlier. Jonathan Fulford, a Yorkshire amateur with a two-round score of 136, spread-eagled the qualifying field in 1983. In 1991 Chris Moody set a course record of 62.

In 2004 an amendment to the qualifying system, introduced a number of final qualifying competitions in this country and abroad. This led to the number of spots left for local final qualifying being much reduced. Consequently, big name players, particularly from overseas, seldom appear at this stage, which is now mainly contested by lower ranked tournament and club professionals along with amateurs.

Club professionals can no longer normally compete with the new breed of tournament professionals and the PGA has provided them with their own events. The Glenmuir Club Professional Championship was played at S&A in 2004. Keenly contested by a field restricted to club professionals, the £10,000 first prize was won by Tony Nash, a Cornish professional with a four round total of 270. The well-known names of the European Tour players were absent, as were those of the many other tournament professionals who people the minor tours. Consequently, such events do not attract the television coverage which makes the principal events attractive to the promoters of proprietary clubs, and are therefore still offered to traditional golf clubs. In conjunction with this tournament the Women's Professional Golf Association title was also decided at S&A. Again it was an event that did not attract the leading home, let alone international, professionals.

What of the professionals who have served the members at S&A? After forty-four years of 'loyal and honourable service', Percy Roberts retired in 1953 and members subscribed over £300 to a testimonial fund. Tom Hiley's account for 1948 illustrates how club professionals relied on purchases made by the members for a large part of their income (Fig.116).

Jack McLachlan, who had been the professional at Newcastle, Royal County Down in Northern Ireland, succeeded Percy Roberts. He was the son of a golf professional and he had been brought up as a golfer with his brothers. On the books of Partick Thistle, Jack turned his back on a possible career in football for golf after reaching the final of the Scottish Boys' Championship. Following service as an assistant at Turnberry and Royal Lytham, for which he received no wages and was supported by his parents, his first post as a professional was at Kilmarnock, from where he moved to Northern Ireland. The board outside his shop at S&A revealed that he had been a winner and

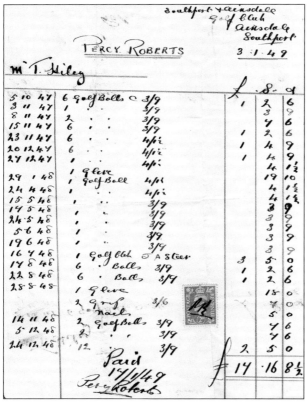

116. *Tom Hiley's account with Percy Roberts 1949.*

twice runner-up in the Irish PGA Championship, along with successes in other events in the province. Something of a specialist bridesmaid, Jack was runner-up seven times in the Ulster Championship. He did, however, win the Hoey Cup, a competition for professionals with Irish clubs, and was elected Captain of the Irish PGA in 1951. Although a good player, with a magical short game, he played little after his arrival at S&A.

Jack ran a well-stocked shop (Fig.117). He thought that it was important to get to know the members and he obtained permission to collect the entry fees for competitions. He attempted to cater for the ladies and, recognising that they would require a different style of merchandising, he installed a large mirror in the shop.

His shop became a nursery for professional golfers. During his time at S&A he saw twenty-six of his assistants move on to take up appointments at other clubs. He brought with him Jim Parkinson who later moved to a post in New Zealand. An early assistant was John Donoghue, who, after six years with Jack, was to become the long-serving professional at Hesketh. John came to the profession through a time-honoured route, acting as a part-time caddie before leaving school, and then becoming an assistant. George Tomlinson, who lived in Liverpool Road close to the clubhouse, followed John as the S&A assistant. George was one of four brothers, all former S&A caddies, who became professional golfers. Elder brother Bill had been an assistant to Percy Roberts. George left for a post at Hindley Hall in 1973 and was succeeded by another local boy - Mike Houghton, who had been a junior

117. Jack McLachlan in his shop.

member of the Southport Old Links Club. In the following year he left to take an appointment at Shaw Hill, Chorley.

In 1974 the Irish PGA honoured Jack McLachlan by making him an honorary member. Jack retired from S&A in the following year, having previously starting to contribute a golf page to the *Southport Visiter*. He obviously had a literary bent and had always enjoyed writing poetry. His golf page included features of local and national interest and competition and match results from the local clubs. Members subscribed over £1,000 for his retirement gift, and he continued to live in the area and enjoy his venture into journalism.

Ian Murdoch, another professional from Newcastle, Royal County Down, replaced Jack and employed his two assistants, Michael Mawdsley and Peter Irving. Despite an expensive makeover of the shop, he never really settled into the post and resigned in 1976. Mike Houghton, who had moved on to Hindley Hall, then returned to take the post at S&A. His golfing career was going well and, in his first year at S&A he qualified for the Open and won the Lancashire Professional Championship. He later won the Lancashire Professional Matchplay Championship and the Liverpool Open Championship. He brought his assistant Paul Shepherd with him from Hindley Hall and continued to employ Michael Mawdsley. Other S&A assistants have included Matthew Chicken, Fraser Fletcher, Jonathan Grogan, John Haliwell, Malcolm Harrison, Roger Livesley, Danny Lloyd, Gary Nelson, Simon Tarr, Max Taylor, Lloyd Tee, Danny Vickers and Matthew Webb.

118. Mike Houghton receives his retirement presentation from Captain Alan Ravey in 2001.

Not all the professionals who graduated from S&A did so through the traditional route. In the late 1970s Neil Brazell was a junior then a colt who went on to win a golf scholarship in America. He was the first S&A golfer to receive scratch status under the new handicap regulations and as an amateur he won several regional events. In 1984, Mike Houghton temporarily employed him, and he later achieved modest success as a tournament professional. Stephen Rooke had an outstanding golf career as a junior and colt at S&A before becoming an assistant at Hillside, where he was also a member. He later became the professional at Windermere. The zenith of his golfing career probably came with an excellent performance in the Open Championship at Carnoustie; whilst the nadir was undoubtedly the severe illness he contracted as a result of playing a course that had recently been sprayed with insecticide. Raife Hutt, another S&A member achieved international success as an amateur before becoming an assistant at Royal Birkdale. After a promising start to his professional career, including a win in the Leeds Challenge Cup, the old north regional professional tournament, the early momentum was not maintained. Raife moved on to a post of teaching professional in Switzerland.

119. Jim Payne and Jack Nicklaus – the Open Championship 1991.

Selected from a field of over sixty applicants, Jim Payne became S&A's professional in 2002, when Mike Houghton retired (Fig.118). He had turned professional after a distinguished amateur career, in which the winning of the Silver Medal as the leading amateur in the 1991 Open Championship at Royal Birkdale was probably the highlight. The runner-up for the medal was Phil Mickelson and Jim enjoyed the unforgettable experience of playing his final round with Jack Nicklaus (Fig.119). In the same year he won the British Youth Championship and the European Amateur Championship. In the following year he won the Sir Henry Cotton Award as the Rookie of the Year on the European Tour. In 1993 he won the Balearic Championship and three years later the Italian Open (Fig.120). It was in this year that he was selected to play for the English team in the World Championship. As a professional he qualified for the Open Championship on three occasions. Despite these tournament successes Jim decided to quit the tour and, after taking his PGA examinations for club professionals, accept the challenge of being the professional at S&A, thus becoming the sixth man to hold this post in the Club's first hundred years.

120. Jim Payne winner of the Italian Open 1996.

Although his priority is now his role as a club professional, his enjoyment of the challenge of tournament golf has led him to play in a number of regional events. Results reflect that he is still a player of considerable ability. An enterprising professional, Jim had to conduct his business from a container on the car park during the building work of 2004. He now has a new, well appointed, strategically placed shop. Here, supported by his assistants, he is continuing to build his business and attempting to be proactive in developing his involvement with members.

Jim launched an unusual initiative in 2004, when he was the joint founder of the 'Prestige Tour'. This was a club for amateur players '…who appreciate the traditions and history of some of the greatest courses in the United Kingdom.' Membership of the club affords the opportunities to play competitive golf on courses such as S&A and Formby. Interestingly the club's itinerary also includes Moortown, the venue of the first Ryder Cup match to be played in this country.

Speaking at his retirement dinner in 2004, John Donoghue, the Hesketh professional who had been an assistant at S&A in the 1950s, suggested that when two club professionals met in his early days, they asked each other about how their game was, but nowadays they ask 'How's business?'

Chapter Nine

CENTENARY POSTSCRIPT

Few clubs have made the impact on the game of golf that Southport & Ainsdale has achieved in its first 100 years. The two initial letters of its name are sufficient to identify it as the club, which twice hosted one of international golf's most prestigious events - the Ryder Cup. For many years the S&A course has provided a competitive challenge for all the great names of professional golf, a role it continued to fulfil until the professional game took a new direction, forsaking the historic classic courses of members' clubs, to play on the recently manufactured layouts of commercial promoters.

It is, however, still possible to see first class golf played at S&A. The quality of amateur golf has never been as high as it presently is, with many young players regarding top amateur championship and representative golf as an apprenticeship for entry into professional tournament golf, rather than time spent as an assistant in a professional's shop. Amateur events, organised by the Royal and Ancient Club, the English Golf Union and the Lancashire Union, continue to be played on members' courses, such as S&A. The championship of the Lancashire Union, a tournament that forms such a significant part of the Club's history, is regularly played at S&A and 2005 saw the Club sharing with Royal Birkdale in mounting Britain's most prestigious amateur event – the Amateur Championship (Fig.121). In the previous year the Club had hosted a schools' international match.

The hosting of tournament golf is only one part of the Club's rich history. Perhaps S&A's strongest claim to fame is the success of individual members and the Club team in representative golf. The trail was blazed by the exploits of Sam Robinson in the 1920s and 1930s. Not only can the Club be proud of his achievements, it can take pride in the fact that this 'artisan golfer' was so warmly welcomed as a member at a time when such recruitment was at least unusual.

The post World War Two period saw the Club enjoy an unrivalled period of regional dominance. The scratch squad was headed up by a group of outstanding international achievers. For a club to have such members is occasion for pride, to have the number who represented S&A, and for so many to be home grown talents, sets S&A apart from almost any other club. This success was grounded in the manner in which the Club nurtured young talent in its boys' and colts' sections. The Club is proud not only in the

121. The Amateur Championship Trophy on the putting green 2005.

golfing achievements of these youngsters, but in the way they were helped to mature into adults who contributed to their club, to golf generally and to wider society. It is a matter of considerable pride that two of them should have become captains of the Royal and Ancient Golf Club of St Andrews.

The Ladies' Section also enjoyed a golden spell in the 1950s and 1960s, with the leading role being played by Welsh international Marjorie Barron. At other times, the standard of ladies' golf at S&A has been creditable without being distinguished. After an early period when S&A was unusually an open club for ladies, membership has been largely restricted to the wives and daughters of members. Such limitation, although common, can have an inhibiting effect on the golfing standards achieved. At S&A some provision was made to admit lower handicap lady golfers without family affiliation to a male member. Perhaps the enlightened attitudes displayed by the Board in developing men's golf did not always extend to the ladies' section. Happily the introduction of an equity policy has now provided the basis for S&A to move forward as a unit. Nevertheless, like so many other clubs, the ladies face a formidable task in attempting to recruit and to retain girls as members.

167

From the 1930s the Club has afforded opportunities for working men to play golf in its Artisan Section, in return for performing duties on the course. It is interesting to note that the artisans too had a golden golfing patch during the same post-war period that ladies' and gentlemen's golf was so strong in the Club.

S&A has evolved from a club leasing a small rough nine-hole course into one that owns one of the country's top golf courses. In 1991 Robert Trent Jones Jnr. visited it as one of a party of forty leading American course architects touring this country. Writing in *Golf World* he described S&A as the best-designed course he had ever played. A 2002 survey undertaken by this magazine placed it in the top hundred courses in the British Isles, two years later a similar survey, undertaken by *Golf Monthly*, had S&A at number thirty-five. S&A's superbly presented and highly rated championship course is one of the golfing jewels amongst the links which make up south-west Lancashire's 'Golf Coast'. The Club has also

122. The dining room 2005.

received an English Golf Environmental Award, in its Centenary Year, in recognition of its dedication to ecological good practice, a tribute to the sensitive work of Dr. Brian Gill and his Green Committee and the course manager, Mike Mercer and his staff.

S&A now also boasts an extended and refurbished clubhouse to match the excellence of the course (Fig.122). It is an elite golf club and each generation of its members has passed its inheritance on with the status of the Club enhanced.

In 2006 the Club will enjoy its long-planned centenary under the leadership of its Captain Paul Gwynne and Lady Captain Carol Fitzgibbon. The highlight will be six days of celebrations in June. Special men's, ladies', mixed and junior competitions will be played and a marquee will house a series of dinners, culminating in a Gala Dinner and Dance on the Saturday. The ladies will be playing for a new Centenary Medal. This trophy has been made from the silver spoons won by the late Mrs. W.J. Harris (lady captain in 1972) and her daughter Mrs. B.J. Joyce (lady captain in 1981).

The men also will have a new centennial trophy which will be known as the Michael Edwards Medal. Michael and the Club have also been honoured, in this Centenary Year, by his having been invited to be the president of the Lancashire Union of Golf Clubs.

The Centenary Year will see the Club hosting the British Mid-Amateur Championship for the Logan Trophy, an event for the more mature players (over thirty-five-years of age) who have not left the amateur game early to face the challenge of competing in the professional game. This is the competition in which S&A member Alan Harrison so distinguished himself in 2005. At the other end of the age spectrum the Schools and Youth Championships will also be played at S&A.

This book demonstrates that S&A is a club with a very distinguished past. The appointment of Tony Crane as Club Historian means that the clubhouse is now used to reflect this history. What is it that the history of the Club's first one hundred years tells us? Above all else, it is that S&A is a 'Golfers' Club' and is one of which its members can be justifiably proud.

123. Back to the welcome of the clubhouse.

Bibliography

Alliss, Peter (ed.),   *Golf – A Way of Life: An Illustrated History,* (1987)

Browning, R.H.K.,   *The Southport and Ainsdale Golf Club: Official Handbook,* (1935, 1953 & 1968)

Childs, W., (mss.),   *Notes on the Origin and Early History of Southport and Ainsdale Golf Club,* (1946)

Concannon, D.,   *The Ryder Cup,* (2002)

Cotton, Henry,   *This Game of Golf,* (1948)

Davies, Patricia,   *A History of Formby Ladies' Golf Club,* (1996)

Dickinson, S., (mss.),   *Origin and Early History of Southport and Ainsdale Golf Club,* (1978)

Dixon, Nancy,   *Hesketh Ladies,* (1989)

Edwards, L.,   *The West Lancashire Golf Club, Blundellsands,* (1973)

Foster, Harry,   *Links Along the Line: The Story of the Development of Golf Between Southport and Liverpool,* (1995)

Foster, Harry,   *Annals of the Hesketh Golf Club 1885-2000,* (2001)

Grant, R. & Hobbs, M.,   'Enter Gloria – with one club and strange clothes', *Golf World* , April 1988.

Hilton, Harold,   *'Where to Golf' ABC Guide to Towns and Pleasure Resorts upon the Lancashire and Yorkshire Railway,* (c.1910)

Irlam, Philip,   *Hillside Golf Club 1911-1991,* (1993)

Johnson, A.J.D.,   *The Royal Birkdale Golf Club,* (1989)

Linacre, J.,   *Southport and Ainsdale Golf Club Official Handbook,* (1922)

MacAlindin, Bob,   *James Braid Champion Golfer,* (2003)

Mair, Lewine,   *One Hundred Years of Women's Golf,* (1992)

Nicklaus, Jack,   *Jack Nicklaus: My Story,* (1997)

Nickson, E.A.,   *The Lytham Century and Beyond 1886-2000,* (2000)

Pitt, N.,   'The Boldest Swinger in Town', *Sunday Times Magazine,* 7th March 2004.

Roberts, Geoffrey, (ed.),   *The Ryder Cup 1933,* (1991)

Roberts, Geoffrey, (mss.),   *A History of Southport and Ainsdale Golf Club,* (1999)

Sefton Coast Life Project,   *Southport and Ainsdale Golf Club: Site management Plan for Golfers and Wildlife,* (1998)

Sommers, Robert,   *The U.S. Open: Golf's Ultimate Challenge,* (1987)

Sommers, Robert,   *Golf Anecdotes,* (1995)

Thomas, I.S.,   *Formby Golf Club 1884-1972,* (1972)

Tiffany, Sylvia,   *Lancashire Ladies County Golf Association: 100 Years 1900-2000,* (1999)

Wilson, E.,   *A Gallery of Women Golfers,* (1961)

Wilson, M. & Bowden, K. (eds.),   *The Best of Henry Longhurst,* (1979)

S&A Golf Club,   *Minutes of the Board, Green, Handicap (Golf Administration), House, Social, Strategic and Finance Committees,* (1906-2006)

Southport Reference Library, *Southport Visiter,* (1906-2006)

                              Proceedings of the Southport Town Council

The Honours Board

Captains

1907 F.W. Smith	1940 W. Bloor	1973 E.J. Simms
1908 S.J.F. Murphy	1941 A. Bradley Dixon	1974 D.F. Ritchie
1909 D.J. Mullholland	1942 A.B. Dawson	1975 G.A. Wade
1910 W. Williamson	1943 F. Orr	1976 W.J. Harris
1911 E. Blackburn	1944 L. Birkett	1977 J.G. Graham
1912 W. Parry	1945 L. Birkett	1978 J. Brennan
1913 T. Mawdsley	1946 J.A. Sloan	1979 J.V. Cubbon
1914 G. Boycott	1947 J.A. Sloan	1980 J. Wilson
1915 A. Appleton	1948 J. Moore	1981 E.J. Williams
1916 H.W. Andrews	1949 G.S. Butler	1982 R.W. Preston
1917 W.J. Yates	1950 T.W. Barker	1983 M. Edwards
1918 G. Roscoe	1951 I.G.W. Newington	1984 H. Beddows
1919 F.S. Yates	1952 J.T. Watts	1985 R.N. Backhouse
1920 F. Lomax	1953 H. Cameron Booth	1986 M.A. Bennett
1921 F.T. Hargreave	1954 E.C. Hoesli	1987 J.V. O'Rourke
1922 J. Crompton	1955 J.J. Smith	1988 A.R. Greaves
1923 E. Blackburn Jnr.	1956 A.R. Ball	1989 P.W. Lennon
1924 E.C. Taylor	1957 C.S. Cullen	1990 P.S. Joyce
1925 T.S. McKenzie	1958 F. Brewer	1991 H.F. Waterson
1926 R.J. Ridout	1959 H. Murphy	1992 I. White
1927 A.P. Douglas	1960 J. Bonar Wood	1993 P. Wilding
1928 J. Lawrie	1961 H. Standish	1994 K. Ritchie
1929 H. Stevens	1962 L. Bowen	1995 S.F. Jackson
1930 H. Stevens	1963 A.E. Charnley	1996 D.J. Ball
1931 A.T. Marcroft	1964 T.M. Bunting	1997 W.P. Whinnett
1932 A.T. Marcroft	1965 R.F. Hardiman	1998 L.D. Morgan
1933 P. Carter	1966 C.B. Smith	1999 M. Attenborough
1934 E.P. Taylor	1967 Dr. D.M. Marsh	2000 R. Draper
1935 J. Marshall	1968 C.G. Erskine	2001 A.J. Ravey
1936 H. Prestt	1969 W.E. Wilding	2002 C.B. Walker
1937 H. Prestt	1970 J.R. Gregory	2003 G.O. Thomas
1938 F. Crewe Roden	1971 S. Dickinson	2004 G.C. Fisher
1939 W. Bloor	1972 J.R. Walker	2005 E. Cheesman

Honorary Life Members (men)

1907 C.J. Skitt	1956 A.B. Dawson
1924 J. Linacre	1966 Dr. D.M. Marsh
1925 S. Robinson	1973 D. Rawlinson
1933 P. Roberts	1983 W. Almond
1951 G.P. Roberts	1983 M. Hargreaves
1953 E.P. Taylor	

Lady Captains

1907 Mrs F.W. Smith	1946 Mrs F. Orr	1976 Mrs A.B. Naylor
1908 Mrs G.J. Harford	1947 Mrs R.F. Pollard	1977 Mrs E. Ball
1909 Mrs G.J. Harford	1948 Mrs R. Nutall	1978 Mrs D. Ritchie
1910 Miss E.K. Mills	1949 Mrs E. Allan	1979 Mrs J.V. Burley
1911 Mrs N.C. Myer	1950 Mrs F. Brewer	1980 Mrs E.J. Simms
1912 Mrs A.B. Crompton	1951 Mrs H. Bitcliffe	1981 Mrs B.J. Joyce
1913 Miss L. Taylor	1952 Mrs S.W. Almond	1982 Mrs J. Gwynne
1914 – 1919	1953 Mrs. E. A. Smith	1983 Mrs R.C. Ellis
1920 Mrs A.B. Crompton	1954 Mrs F.A. Smith	1984 Mrs J. Wilson
1921 Mrs F.T. Hargreave	1955 Mrs R.A. Basford	1985 Mrs J.G. Graham
1922 Mrs T.S. McKenzie	1956 Mrs C.S. Cullen	1986 Mrs D. Dickinson
1923 Mrs A.F. Myer	1957 Mrs H. Murphy	1987 Mrs D. Rimmer
1924 Mrs A.P. Douglas	1958 Mrs H. Murphy	1988 Mrs F.E. Greaves
1925 Mrs C.H. Hesketh	1959 Mrs M.A. Reece	1989 Mrs M.E. Bennett
1926 Miss S. Mawdesley	1960 Mrs T.B. Clarkson	1990 Mrs A. Proudley
1927 Miss M. Hesketh	1961 Mrs C. Hinns	1991 Mrs H. Wilson
1928 Mrs J. Watts	1962 Mrs D.E. Eades	1992 Mrs E.D. Dutton
1929 Miss M. Wren	1963 Mrs H. Wilkinson	1993 Mrs D. Albert
1930 Miss K.A. Jack	1964 Miss W.M. Wilson	1994 Mrs J.M. Cullen
1931 Mrs J.H. Young	1965 Mrs J. Shand	1995 Mrs D. Ravey
1932 Mrs A. Faux	1966 Mrs A.E. Mann	1996 Mrs N. Jenkins
1933 Mrs J. Prestwich	1967 Mrs T.M. Bunting	1997 Mrs E. O'Rourke
1934 Mrs A.B. Dawson	1968 Mrs J.R. Gregory	1998 Mrs E. Joyce
1935 Mrs F. Gorse	1969 Mrs E. Powell	1999 Mrs R. Ritchie
1936 Mrs G. Douglas	1970 Mrs D.M. Marsh	2000 Mrs J.M. Wilding
1937 Mrs S. Yates	1971 Mrs G.C. Bateson	2001 Mrs J. Ball
1938 Mrs S. Holland	1972 Mrs W.J. Harris	2002 Mrs J. Downing
1939 Mrs E. Tomlinson	1973 Mrs J. Baker	2003 Mrs P. Henshaw
1940 – 1944	1974 Mrs E.M. Barker	2004 Mrs S. Bell
1945 Mrs S.W. Morris	1975 Mrs S. Kidger	2005 Mrs L. Nolte

Honorary Life Associate Members (ladies)

1960 Marjorie Barron	1976 Judy Bunting
1968 Annie Sherrington	2003 Dorothy Ritchie
1974 Marjorie Wren	

International and County Honours

English International Players

	Period	Played	Won	Halved	Lost
S. Robinson	1925-1930	8	5	0	3
D. Rawlinson.	1949-1961	30	13	2	15
G.P. Roberts	1949-1951	8	1	0	7
Dr. D.M. Marsh	1956-1972	75	40	7	28
R.A.R. Hutt	1991-1993	23	14	1	8

Irish International Player

M. Edwards	1956-1963	19	13	0	6

Lancashire County Players

S. Robinson	1920-1936	26	14	5	7
E. Blackburn	1921-1926	19	13	0	6
C. Marshall	1926	1	0	0	1
C. Southwell	1927-1932	8	4	0	4
C. Mackenzie	1928-1932	5	5	0	0
F. Hargreave	1930	2	0	0	2
A. Bothwell	1934-1952	4	1	1	2
E.T. Darrah	1936-1938	6	2	1	3
T. Hiley	1938-1960	41	21	3	17
J.T. Shiel	1947-1951	10	2	2	6
D. Rawlinson	1948-1975	101	56	9	36
G.P. Roberts	1948-1964	22	9	1	12
J.R. Wroe	1950-1970	43	15	4	24
I.G.W. Newington	1950	1	0	0	1
R.S. Nichols	1950	1	0	0	1
Dr. D.M. Marsh	1955-1975	48	23	9	16
J.H.M. Williams	1968	1	0	1	0
M. Edwards	1970-1975	19	13	4	2
W.S.M. Rooke	1970-1974	17	6	1	10
B.P. Williams	1975-1981	25	10	3	12
F.G. Till	1978	2	0	0	2
P.A. Bagshaw	1986-	18	5	4	9
R.A.R. Hutt	1989-1993	30	17	4	9
P.J. Bird	1995-	9	4	1	4
M. Bailey	1997-	7	3	0	4

Other S&A members have played for Lancashire, but are listed by the county as members of their other clubs.

Sam Robinson Trophy

(Lowest nett aggregate for six cards)

1950 D. Rawlinson	1969 P. Green	1989 M. Attenborough
1951 J.R. Wroe	1970 J.R. Wroe	1990 P.J. Green
1952 S.W. Almond	1971 D. Birch	1991 T. Rawlings
1953 J.J. Collins	1972 M. Rawlinson	1992 A. Meekin
1954 K.M. Davies	1973 J. Hiley	1993 J. Blackhurst
H. Murphy	1974 H. Drake	1994 C. Sawyer
1955 T.M. Bunting	1975 A.N. Reardon	1995 I. McLelland
1956 G.F. Bourne	1976 F.M. Hargeave	1996 G. Fallows
1957 F.C. Jones	1977 D. Henwood	1997 J.J. Fleetwood
1958 W. Hall	1978 E. Ball	1998 M. Bailey
1959 D. Rawlinson	E. Boileau	1999 A.W. Harrison
1960 D. Rawlinson	P. Rimmer	2000 N. McAulay
1961 G.P. Roberts	1979 J.J. Barber	2001 A.W. Harrison
1962 J.R.S. Eccles	1980 M. Rawlinson	2002 I.R. Leadbetter
1963 T. Hiley	1981 K. Wright	2003 M. Godfrey
1964 J.C. Bailey	1982 R.K. Pegg	2004 I.R. Leadbetter
1965 W. Dean	1983 M. Edwards	2005 A. Maitland
1966 C. Davies	1984 P.A. Bagshaw	
1967 S.B. Brayshaw	1985 B.P. Williams	
M. Rawlinson	1986 P.A. Bagshaw	
1968 R.S. Aukland	1987 A. Jackson	
T.Hiley	1988 I. McLelland	

Dixon Rawlinson Trophy

(Lowest gross aggregate for four rounds of Spring and Autumn Meetings)

1979 G.P. Roberts 311	1989 P.A. Bagshaw 299	1998 P.S. Platt 303
1980 M. Edwards 312	1990 B.P. Williams 311	1999 A. Eden 289
1981 R.B. Williams 317	1991 P.A. Bagshaw 311	2000 A.W. Harrison 301
1982 N.R.W. Lucas 306	1992 P.A. Bagshaw 289	2001 A.W. Harrison 290
1983 M. Edwards 293	1993 P.A. Bagshaw 299	2002 P.A. Bagshaw 294
1984 M. Edwards 317	C.I. Middleton 299	A.W. Harrison 294
1985 P.J. Green 311	1994 P.A. Bagshaw 313	2003 J. Rodwell 297
N.R.W. Lucas 311	P. Green 313	2004 P.J. Bird 301
1986 A. Jackson 300	1995 P.J. Bird 296	2005 P.J. Bird 302
1987 P.A. Bagshaw 302	1996 M. O'Brien 301	
1988 C.I. Middleton 323	1997 M. Bailey 300	

David Marsh Trophy

(Lowest nett aggregate for four rounds of the Spring and Autumn meetings)

1971	M. Edwards	1984	A.C. Horne		J. Fleetwood
1972	C. Davies	1985	D.J. Midghall	1997	R.B. Williams
1973	D. Henwood	1986	A. Jackson	1998	P.S. Platt
1974	P.J. Green	1987	P.A. Bagshaw	1999	M.A. Cunningham
	J. Wright	1988	C.I. Middleton	2000	G.C. Williams
1975	A.E. Brook	1989	C.I. Middleton	2001	A.W. Harrison
1976	P.J. Green	1990	L. Eastham	2002	A.W. Harrison
1977	M. Edwards	1991	C. Sawyer		G.J. Fallows
1978	D. Rawlinson	1992	P.A. Bagshaw	2003	R. McBride
1979	P. Conning	1993	C. Sawyer		M.K. Pymm
1980	M. Edwards	1994	T. Lawton	2004	G.C. Fisher
1981	P. Jackson	1995	M.A. Jenkins	2005	M. Till
1982	E. Bray	1996	M. O'Brien		
1983	G.P. Roberts		G. Williams		

Tom Bunting Trophy

(Lowest 36 hole nett score in the Autumn Meeting)

1976	N.R.W. Lucas	1986	A. Simpkin	1996	A.C. Horne
1977	M. Edwards	1987	P.A. Bagshaw	1997	R.B. Williams
1978	G.P. Roberts	1988	C.I. Middleton	1998	J. Blackhurst
1979	D. Platt	1989	F.G. Till	1999	M.P. Jackson
1980	H. Bond	1990	J.M. Morrison	2000	D. Pilkington
1981	E. Ball	1991	A.M. Proudley	2001	A.W. Harrison
1982	D.N. Culshaw	1992	P.A. Bagshaw	2002	A.W. Harrison
1983	G. Regan	1993	P.B. Gwynne	2003	J. Earl
1984	A.C. Horne	1994	M.A. Cunningham	2004	R. Sturgeon
1985	J.A. Davies	1995	M.A. Jenkins	2005	G. Middleton

Captain's Prize

(Match Play Knockout)

1907	W.H. Child	1940	T. Hiley	1973	T. Lloyd
1908	W. Sugg	1941	T. Hiley	1974	B.H. Crabtree
1909	S.J.F. Murphy	1942	S. Robinson	1975	S. Child
1910	S.J.F. Murphy	1943	S. Atkinson	1976	P. Hiley
1911	D.J. Mulholland	1944	C.W. Davies	1977	G.P. Roberts
1912	J.E. Fieldhouse	1945	G. Little	1978	D.M. Marsh
1913	W. Nutall	1946	S. Yates	1979	R.K. Pegg
1914	E. Blackburn	1947	S. Robinson	1980	D.M. Marsh
1915	T. Mawdesley	1948	A. B. Naylor	1981	J.J. Barber
1916	E. Heywood	1949	A. Bothwell	1982	M. Edwards
1917	H.T. Robens	1950	S. Robinson	1983	S. Mattinson
1918	J. Crompton	1951	D.M. Marsh	1984	F.G. Till
1919	E. Wilkinson	1952	S. Yates	1985	J.J. Barber
1920	R.J. Ridout	1953	D.M. Marsh	1986	R.W. Greaves
1921	W.S. Dutton	1954	D. Rawlinson	1987	M. Hall
1922	G. Baird	1955	G.F. Bourne	1988	T. Rawlings
1923	A.H. Parker	1956	H. Cameron Booth	1989	K.C. Kidger
1924	F. Lomax	1957	J.G. Graham	1990	P.A. Bagshaw
1925	F.T. Hargreave	1958	G.P. Roberts	1991	J.J. Large
1926	F. Fraser	1959	D.M. Marsh	1992	P. Shawcross
1927	S.W. Almond	1960	G.P. Roberts	1993	T.P. Culshaw
1928	S. Robinson	1961	J.R. Wroe	1994	P. Shawcross
1929	K. Koller	1962	W.R. Titmarsh	1995	T. Rawlings
1930	S. Yates	1963	D. Rawlinson	1996	M. Jackson
1931	J.H. Boyd	1964	A.J. Colclough	1997	P.J. Bird
1932	S. Robinson	1965	R. Raby	1998	A.W. Harrison
1933	R.S. Perkins	1966	T. Hiley	1999	P.J. Bird
1934	R.S. Perkins	1967	A.N. Buckles	2000	W.E. Guest
1935	K. Koller	1968	T. Hiley	2001	P.J. Bird
1936	I.G.W. Newington	1969	T. Hiley	2002	R.K. Pegg
1937	E.T. Darrah	1970	P.E. Morris	2003	M. Baxter
1938	J.J. Preston	1971	A.E. Charnley	2004	M.Till
1939	G.F. Bell	1972	J. Hardman	2005	G. Cooper

Scratch Prize

(Lowest thirty-six hole gross score in the Autumn Meeting)

1913	T. Mawdesley	80	1948	D. Rawlinson	75	1978	D.M. Marsh	146
1914	T. Mawdesley	84	1949	D. Rawlinson	73	1979	D.M. Marsh	146
1915	H. Eastwood	82	1950	D. Rawlinson	149	1980	N.R.W. Lucas	153
1916	T. Mawdesley	75	1951	D. Rawlinson	144	1981	P.J. Green	153
1917	J. Crompton	86	1952	J.R. Wroe	157	1982	N.R.W. Lucas	148
1918	J. Crompton	90	1953	D. Rawlinson	144	1983	M. Edwards	146
1919	E. Blackburn	87	1954	D. Rawlinson	150	1984	B.P. Williams	156
1920	S. Robinson	75	1955	T. Hiley		1985	N.R.W. Lucas	151
1921	S. Robinson	75	1956	D. Rawlinson	145	1986	N.R.W. Lucas	152
1922	S. Robinson	73	1957	G.P. Roberts	143	1987	P.A. Bagshaw	146
1923	T. Mawdesley	81	1958	T. Hiley	147	1988	P.G. Till	152
1924	S. Robinson	76	1959	G.P. Roberts	145	1989	A. Jackson	143
1925	H. Koller	82	1960	T. Hiley	148	1990	R.A.R. Hutt	146
1926	S. Robinson	73	1961	J.R. Wroe	149	1991	P.A. Bagshaw	151
1927	S. Robinson	72	1962	T. Hiley	144	1992	P.A. Bagshaw	140
1928	C. Mackenzie	77	1963	D. Rawlinson	150	1993	P.A. Bagshaw	148
1929	S. Robinson	73	1964	T. Hiley	145	1994	M. O'Brien	154
1930	S. Robinson	72	1965	G.P. Roberts	149	1995	P.A. Bagshaw	150
1931	S. Robinson	76	1966	D. Rawlinson	152	1996	A.C. Horne	145
1932	F. Brewer	76	1967	D.M. Marsh	142	1997	A. Eden	140
1933			1968	D.M. Marsh	145	1998	P.A. Bagshaw	149
1934	S. Robinson	70	1969	T. Hiley	147	1999	A. Eden	140
1935	S. Robinson	75	1970	D.H.D. Forsyth	149	2000	G.T. Gillespie	149
1936	S. Robinson	72	1971	D.M. Marsh	145	2001	A.W. Harrison	143
1937	S. Robinson	70	1972	M. Edwards	147	2002	A.W. Harrison	139
1938	F. Brewer	78	1973	M. Edwards	148	2003	J. Rodwell	144
1939	T. Hiley	76	1974	H.E. Swash	149	2004	J. Rodwell	145
1940-1945			1975	M. Edwards	157	2005	M. Rabone	145
1946	J. Telfer Shiel	75	1976	B.P. Williams	151			
1947	D. Rawlinson	75	1977	M. Edwards	154			

Spring Meeting – Scratch Trophy

(Lowest thirty-six hole gross score in the Spring Meeting)

1971	M. Edwards	147	1983	M. Edwards	147	1995	P.J. Bird	144
1972	M. Edwards	146	1984	G.P. Roberts	155	1996	P. Green	149
1973	J.R. Wroe	152	1985	B.P. Williams	155	1997	M. Baily	147
1974	M. Rawlinson	150	1986	A. Jackson	148	1998	P.S. Platt	152
1975	M. Edwards	152	1987	P.A. Bagshaw	156	1999	A.W. Harrison	143
1976	D.H.D. Forsyth	153	1988	P.A. Bagshaw	150	2000	P.S. Platt	142
1977	M. Edwards	152	1989	P.A. Bagshaw	154	2001	P.A. Bagshaw	147
1978	D. Rawlinson	156	1990	I.A. Proudley	157	2002	P.J. Bird	147
1979	G.P. Roberts	152	1991	B.P. Williams	156	2003	A.W. Harrison	148
1980	M. Edwards	145	1992	P.A. Bagshaw	149	2004	A. Butcher	151
1981	B.P. Williams	155	1993	C.I. Middleton	147	2005	P.A. Bagshaw	153
1982	K. Green	151	1994	P. Green	152			

St. Dunstans Competition

(Eighteen hole Medal)

1920 E. Heywood	1949 B.E. Byers	1978 M.A. Bennett
1921 N. Coppock	1950 C.G.P. Alliston	1979 N.R.W. Lucas
1922 J.F. McKenzie	1951 S. Moran	1980 E. Boileau
1923 H. Bleasdale	1952 G.C. Erskine	1981 D.M. Marsh
1924 J.A. Hardie	1953 C.G. Pallinston	1982 C.W. Metcalfe
1925 J. Fraser	1954 D. Rawlinson	1983 G.P. Hatch
1926 D.W. Hutton	1955 J.R.J.M. Marsh	1984 I. Gregson
1927 R. Mackenzie	1956 H.W. Moorman	1985 J.R. Watson
1928 C. Southwell	1957 W. Smith	1986 R. Duce
1929 E.T. Darrah	1958 C.B. Sunderland	1987 M.R. Schofield
1930 S.W. Almond	1959 F.O. Bassett	1988 E. Howard
1931 E. Coleby	1960 G. Staveley-Dick	1989 J. London
1932 F. Hopkinson	1961 A.N. Buckley	1990 P.C. Underwood
1933 J. Lawrie	1962 R.H. Phayre	1991 J.R. Pickup
1934 J. Pearson	1963 J. Wright	1992 D.D.M. Brookes
1935 J.F. Shawcross	1964 B.S. Thomas	1993 J. Mottram
1936 B.F. Gill	1965 G.E. Chidley	1994 S. Tasker
1937 J.H. Ward	1966 E.J. Simms	1995 H. Ankers
1938 O.A. Heath	1967 D.H.D. Forsyth	1996 M. Godfrey
1939 G.F. Bell	1968 D. Rawlinson	1997 C. Sawyer
1940 C.H. Lamb	1969 G.C. Jones	1998 M. Attenborough
1941 J.G. Lugton	1970 R. Ewing	1999 J. Rodwell
1942 R.F. Pollard	1971 D. Rawlinson	2000 P.J. Halsall
1943 I.G.W. Newington	1972 G.M.J. Bourne	2001 W.F. Riley
1944 B. Hepton	1973 J.R.J.M. Marsh	2002 B.P. Williams
1945 F. Brewer	1974 I.G.W. Newington	2003 D. Buck
1946 J. Moore	1975 R.N. Groves	2004 A.C. Horne
1947 A.B. Naylor	1976 R. Jones	2005 I. McIlroy
1948 C.B. Sutherland	1977 C.J. Hicks	

178

Peace Trophy

(Lowest nett score over 36 holes)

1919 F. Blomley	1952 L. Birkett	1979 D. Keeley
1920 A. Oxley	1953 S.T. Leach	1980 J.G. Graham
1921 D.W. Hutton	1954 C.B. Sunderland	1981 J. Greaves
1922 S.M. Yates	1955 C.B. Smith	1982 D. Hindle
1923 T.S. McKenzie	1956 R.N. Evans	1983 D. Callow
1924 G. Little	1957 J.R. Bather	1984 I.A. Proudley
1925 G. Douglas	1958 W. Hall	1985 N. McQueen
1926 S. Robinson	1959 D. Rawlinson	1986 R.J. Howard
1927 C. McKenzie	1960 J.R.S. Eccles	1987 A. Jackson
1928 H. Koller	1961 A.E. Charnley	1988 D.J. Midghall
1929 J. Crompton	1962 W. Dean	1989 G.C. Fisher
1930 A.W. Knights	1963 R.J. Basford	1990 P.J. Green
1931 C. Moores	1964 K. Bennett	1991 A.N. Reardon
1932 J. Marshall	1965 S.K. Thomas	1992 J. Large
1933 T.S. McKenzie	1966 F.K. Marriner	1993 J. Kirkness
1934 T.S. McKenzie	1967 H. Beddows	1994 H.B.R. Williams
1935 A. Lee Wilkins	1968 N. You	1995 C. Grimley
1936 J. Moores	1969 D.J. Simms	1996 R. Sturgeon
1937 J.F. Woods	1970 R. Halliday	1997 J.B. Underwood
1938 A.B. Dawson	1971 R.S.M. Rooke	1998 A.G. Halsall
1939 C.D. Northrop	1972 H. Mattinson	1999 M.A. Jenkins
1946 R.A. Spedding	1973 A. Rushton	2000 D. Pilkington
1947 L.A. Webber	1974 D.W. Culshaw	2001 P.A. Bagshaw
1948 G.C. Erskine	1975 H.E. Swash	2002 I.R. Leadbetter
1949 J.J. Smith	1976 D.P. Smith	2003 R.W. Greaves
1950 A. Bothwell	1977 V.J. Brooks	2004 A.W. Harrison
1951 F. Brewer	1978 J.R. Halsall	2005 R.W. Greaves

Blackburn Holden Cup

(Lowest thirty-six hole nett score in the Spring Meeting)

1910 W.H. Child	1940-1946	1976 J.R. Walker
1911 B. Lunt	1947 B.N. Hepton	1977 P.S. Joyce
1912 C. Hesketh	1948 A. Bruce Naylor	1978 P. Dean
1913 T. Dransfield	1949 J.R.J.M. Marsh	1979 G.P. Roberts
1914 H.F. Tomlinson	1950 H. Murphy	1980 C. Leroy
1915 S.C. Parker	1951 R.H. Boyd	1981 R.B. Williams
1916 E.C. Taylor	1952 H. Murphy	1982 E. Bray
1917 J.D. Sutcliffe	1953 R.F. Pollard	1983 M. Edwards
1918 H. Koller	1954 E.C. Bolton	1984 S.D.R. Marsh
1919 H. Whittle	1955 R.N. Evans	1985 D.J. Midghall
1920 S. Robinson	1956 J. Hardman	1986 A. Jackson
1921 C. Mackenzie	1957 W. Hall	1987 R.W. Greaves
1922 S. Robinson	1958 J.S. Yates	1988 R.A.R. Hutt
1923 J. Voce	1959 H. Murphy	1989 G. Fitzgibbon
1924 J. Irving	1960 G.P. Roberts	1990 T.J. Kershaw
1925 C. Southwell	1961 J.R. Basford	1991 J.P. Buck
1926 C. Southwell	1962 F. Deane	1992 R.I. Sawyer
1927 S.W. Almond	1963 P.A. Tickle	1993 D. Smith
1928 W.N. Lewis	1964 M.F.S. Connell	1994 P. Green
1929 F. Bewer	1965 J.R.J.M. Marsh	1995 R.I. Sawyer
1930 J.E. Dyson	1966 B. Toubkin	1996 J. Fazakerly
1931 J.E. West	1967 B. Barber	1997 A.G. Halsall
1932 N. Coppock	1968 M. Rawlinson	1998 M.E. Wilding
1933 J.B. Millward	1969 S. Yates	1999 J.B. Underwood
1934 A. Oswald	1970 M. Edwards	2000 P.S. Platt
1935 C. Moores	1971 M. Edwards	2001 D. Pilkington
1936 A.L. Edwards	1972 M.E. Wilding	2002 G.J. Fallows
1937 C.H. Lamb	1973 A. Lancaster	2003 R. McBride
1938 T.C. Ormrod	1974 M. Rawlinson	2004 G.C. Fisher
1939 R.F. Pollard	1975 W. Hall	2005 M. Till

Ladies' Section - Captain's Prize

1907	L. Taylor	1946	L. Sumner	1976	S. Wright
1908	L. Taylor	1947	H. Biltcliffe	1977	J. Burley
1909	L. Taylor	1948	C. Hinns	1978	A.B. Naylor
1910	L. Taylor	1949	W. Taylor	1979	S. Burnett
1911	-	1950	P. Horrocks	1980	M.A. Reece
1912	F. Evans	1951	M. Barron	1981	J. Gwynne
1913	-	1952	J.P. Richardson	1982	A. McClellan
1914 – 1919		1953	G. Watts	1983	E. Jones
1920	L.Taylor	1954	J.P. Richardson	1984	D. Mayer
1921	S. Haworth	1955	M. Barron	1985	C. Wroe
1922	G.M. Whiteside	1956	M. Barron	1986	N. Jenkins
1923	T.S. McKenzie	1957	F. Orr	1987	J. Cawley
1924	L. Taylor	1958	G. Bourne	1988	C. Wroe
1925	J.H. Watts	1959	H.D. Cousins	1989	J. Wilding
1926	I. Shaw	1960	R.F. Pollard	1990	S. Hutt
1927	C.M. Turner	1961	H. Wilkinson	1991	D. Ravey
1928	T.C. Ormrod	1962	W.L. McCallum	1992	S. Inglis
1929	I. Shaw	1963	J.H. Barke	1993	E. Jones
1930	T.S. McKenzie	1964	E.A. Smith	1994	L. Howard
1931	I. Turner	1965	J.B. Clarkson	1995	E.M. Waterson
1932	F. Gorse	1966	J. Wroe	1996	S. McClachlan
1933	R. Huke	1967	E.A. Smith	1997	D. Ravey
1934	H. Andrew	1968	K. Bennett	1998	E.M. Waterson
1935	M. Wren	1969	W.M. Wilson	1999	P. Beattie
1936	E. Tomlinson	1970	J.R. Gregory	2000	M. Rimmer
1937	I. Shaw	1971	J. Richardson	2001	M. Livermore
1938	W.M. Nelson	1972	J.D. Dickinson	2002	P. Campbell
1939	M. Barron	1973	J.R. Gregory	2003	P. Campbell
1940 –1944		1974	A.B. Naylor	2004	A. Pymm
1945	L. Hoyle	1975	J.B. Gwynne	2005	D. Fletcher

Ladies' Section - Hall (Coronation) Cup

1911 J.C. Morris	1946 I. Shaw	1977 S. Burnett
1912 A.F. Meyer	1947 R. Nuttall	1978 H. Edwards
1913 C. Hesketh	1948 C. Hinns	1979 D. Rimmer
1914 A. B. Crompton	1949 H. Cousins	1980 S. Kidger
1915 L. Taylor	1950 H. Sherrington	1981 H. Bennett
1916 A. Faux	1951 J.K. Kay	1982 J.V. Burley
1917 J. Prestwich	1952 G. Watts	1983 S. Kidger
1918 Mrs. Wilkinson	1953 G. Murrell	1984 B. Naylor
1919 A. Henderson	1954 G.S. Pearson	1985 D. Ravey
1920 M. Wren	1955 G.S. Pearson	1986 E. Jones
1921 J. Crompton	1956 T.S. McKenzie	1987 S. Kidger
1922 G.M. Whiteside	1957 F. Orr	1988 J. Morris
1923 E. Hindley	1958 D. Pearson	1989 B. Dickinson
1924 I. Turner	1959 W.L. McCallum	1990 B. Joyce
1925 M.W. Arthur	1960 W. Hall	1991 H. Wilson
1926 M. Wren	1961 E.A. Smith	1992 J. Downing
1927 E.C. Nolan	1962 D.E. Eades	1993 D. Ravey
1928 G.M. Whiteside	1963 M. Wren	1994 N. Smith
1929 M.E. Sumner	1964 P. Shaw	1995 D. Ravey
1930 I. Turner	1965 J.R. Gregory	1996 J. You
1931 B. Lunt	1966 W. Hall	1997 T. Rimmer
1932 R. Huke	1967 B.J. Harris	1998 M. Livermore
1933 F. Orr	1968 W.J. Harris	1999 J. Wilding
1934 G. Douglas	1969 G.R. Gregory	2000 J. Taylor
1935 G.R. Spencer	1970 E.A. Smith	2001 C. Scully
1936 G.R. Spencer	1971 S. Kidger	2002 E.M. Waterson
1937 I. Shaw	1972 H. Edwards	2003 M.J. Lawton
1938 M. Barron	1973 T.M. Bunting	2004 L. Nolte
1939 M. Williamson	1974 G.C. Bateson	2005 J. Leadbetter
1940 – 1944	1975 B.J. Joyce	
1945 R.F. Pollard	1976 S. Burnett	

Ladies' Section - Scratch Trophy

Year	Name	Score	Year	Name	Score	Year	Name	Score
1950	M.A. Reece	77	1967	M. Barron	80	1986	D. Rimmer	79
1951	M. Barron	75	1968	M. Barron	79	1987	D. Rimmer	82
1952	M. Barron	79		F. Pearson	79	1988	D. Rimmer	83
	M.A. Reece	79	1969	M. Barron	81	1989	L. Fairclough	74
1953	M.A. Reece	77	1970	M. Barron	75	1990	A. Brighouse	77
1954	M. Barron	79	1971	D.M. Marsh	76	1991	T. Marsden	79
	W.L. McCallum	79	1972	D.M. Marsh	81	1992	L. Cheesman	80
1955	M. Barron	77	1973	D.M. Marsh	81	1993	D. Rimmer	81
1956	M. Barron	76	1974	M.A. Reece	78	1994	D. Ravey	81
1957	M. Barron	78	1975	M. Barron	82		A. Raeburn	81
	J. Shand	78	1976	M.A. Reece	82	1995	D. Ravey	77
1958	M. Barron	78	1977	M. Barron	84	1996	E. Jones	79
	J. Shand	78	1978	D. Rimmer	85	1997	D. Ravey	75
1959	M.A. Reece	74	1979	D.Rimmer	83	1998	D. Fletcher	80
1960	J. Shand	75		A. Bateson	83	1999	D. Fletcher	79
1961	M.A. Reece	79	1980	D. Rimmer	82	2000	L. Nolte	82
1962	M. Barron	74	1981	D. Rimmer	79	2001	D. Ravey	80
1963	M. Barron	77	1982	D. Rimmer	82	2002	D. Fletcher	81
1964	M. Barron	75	1983	D. Rimmer	80	2003	D. Fletcher	80
1965	J. Shand	72	1984	D. Mayer	78	2004	L. Nolte	82
1966	M. Barron	70	1985	D. Rimmer	76	2005	D. Ravey	83

Ladies' Section - Match Play Championship

Year	Name	Year	Name	Year	Name
1974	S. Smith	1985	N. Jenkins	1996	N. Jenkins
1975	M. Barron	1986	N. Jenkins	1997	D. Rimmer
1976	J. Alexander	1987	E.M. Waterson	1998	E. Jones
1977	M. Barron	1988	M. Bennett	1999	E.M. Waterson
1978	A. Bateson	1989	N. Smith	2000	D. Ravey
1979	M. Culshaw	1990	N. Culshaw	2001	D. Ravey
1980	J. Gwynne	1991	K. Forbes	2002	B. Bond
1981	B. Greensmith	1992	D. Ravey	2003	L. Nolte
1982	B.J. Joyce	1993	D. Ravey	2004	E. Jones
1983	H. Wilson	1994	D. Ravey	2005	P. Morris
1984	H. Wilson	1995	B. Bond		

Ladies' Section – Millennium Trophy

Year	Name	Year	Name	Year	Name
2000	L. Nolte	2002	C. Grice	2004	P. Kirkham
2001	B. Bond	2003	C. McFarlin	2005	M. Halpin

Ladies' Section - Silver Jubilee Trophy

1977 E. Jones	1987 B. Joyce	1997 S.E. Hutt
1978 E. Jones	1988 D. Graham	1998 J. Downing
1979 S. Burnett	1989 E.M. Waterson	1999 K. Forbes
1980 M. Bennett	1990 S. Inglis	2000 L. Morris
1981 K. Richardson	1991 S. Kennedy	2001 C. Grice
1982 L. Nolte	1992 S. Kidger	2002 C. McGovern
1983 J.M. Cullen	1993 B. Corless	2003 S. McLachlan
1984 D. Mayer	1994 D. Ravey	2004 O. Ennis
1985 B. Joyce	1995 J. Wright	2005 M. Milnes
1986 J. Ball	1996 C. Storer	

Ladies' Section - Marjorie Wren Trophy

1983 D. Dickinson	1991 S. McLachlan	1999 L. Nolte
1984 J. Henderson	1992 S. Inglis	2000 K. Forbes
1985 D. Mayer	1993 D. Ravey	2001 D. Ravey
1986 E. Jones	1994 D. Ravey	2002 M. Rimmer
1987 J. Wright	1995 D. Ravey	2003 M. Rimmer
1988 E. Jones	1996 E. Jones	2004 L. Nolte
1989 L. Fairclough	1997 C. Storer	2005 E. O'Keefe
1990 S. Bell	1998 L. Nolte	

Ladies' Section - Jennifer Marsh Trophy

1985 D. Ravey	222	1993 D. Ravey	224	2000 D. Ravey	223
1986 E. Jones	219	L. Howard	224	2001 L. Nolte	227
1987 J. Wright	229	1994 D. Ravey	218	2002 C. Storer	229
1988 J.G. Graham	228	1995 S. Inglis	220	2003 M. Livermore	222
1989 N. Smith	219	1996 E. Jones	217	2004 P. Rooney	226
1990 I. Appleton	221	1997 M. Livermore	226	2005 J. Towndrow	228
1991 D. Rimmer	217	1998 L. Nolte	227		
1992 J. Ball	224	1999 K. Forbes	225		

Ladies' Section - Gentleman's Captain's Prize

1994 M. Tasker	1998 O. Ennis	2002 P. Jackson
1995 K. Forbes	1999 C.A. McGovern	2003 E.M. Kite
1996 D. Ravey	2000 G. Scully	2004 J. Leadbetter
1997 B. Bond	2001 M. Rimmer	2005 J. Leadbetter

Extract from 6″
Ordnance Survey Map 1926